26 25 24 23 22 21 20   1 2 3 4 5 6 7 8

Hardcover ISBN: 978-1-5064-5915-8
Ebook ISBN: 978-1-5064-6656-9

Cover design: Sara Zarr
Interior design: Kim Winscher
Illustrations: Chelen Ecija

Library of Congress Cataloging-in-Publication Data

Names: Zarr, Sara, author.
Title: Courageous creativity : advice and encouragement for the creative
    life / Sara Zarr.
Description: Minneapolis : Beaming Books, 2020. | Audience: Ages 9-13 |
    Summary: "Expert advice and encouragement are paired with exercises to
    help you face down your fears, let go of expectations, stop comparing
    yourself to others, and make your art with courage"-- Provided by
    publisher.
Identifiers: LCCN 2020007386 (print) | LCCN 2020007387 (ebook) | ISBN
    9781506459158 (hardcover) | ISBN 9781506466569 (ebook)
Subjects: LCSH: Creative ability--Juvenile literature. | Creative ability
    in children--Juvenile literature. | Encouragement--Juvenile literature.
Classification: LCC BF723.C7 Z37 2020  (print) | LCC BF723.C7  (ebook) |
    DDC 153.3/5083--dc23
LC record available at https://lccn.loc.gov/2020007386
LC ebook record available at https://lccn.loc.gov/2020007387

VN0004589; 9781506459158; AUG2020

Beaming Books
510 Marquette Avenue
Minneapolis, MN 55402
Beamingbooks.com

# COURAGEOUS CREATIVITY

## ADVICE and ENCOURAGEMENT FOR THE Creative Life

by SARA ZARR

✳ beaming books
MINNEAPOLIS

# TABLE OF CONTENTS

My name is Sara, and I'm a writer.

I've been writing fiction for over twenty years and have been doing it as my primary job for the last dozen years or so. Along the way, I've learned some things about the business of publishing and the craft of writing. I've taken planes, trains, and automobiles to interesting places to talk about my books and to teach other writers. I've met some of my heroes and made new friends. I've spoken with readers as well as booksellers, teachers, librarians, and parents who love to help young people find their next favorite book.

All of this has been gratifying and unexpected—taking me places I never thought I'd go.

But some of the most interesting stuff I've learned has been about myself. I knew that I'm resourceful and creative, that I love stories, that I have a vivid imagination, and that I love writing. But what I didn't know before about myself but know now is this:

- No matter how much I love writing, it is always extremely difficult to get myself to sit down and do it.

- I'm terrified of being criticized, but I always manage to live through it.

- I really enjoy being around other writers and artists and all types of creative people, and I love having them as friends. But I also experience a lot of envy of other writers and artists—even (and maybe especially) my friends.

- I still have a hard time taking creative risks, even though I know it's an important part of the process.

- I get into creative ruts and get burned out on writing.

- I never feel capable of writing the book I'm writing.

- For some reason, I do it anyway!

- Even after reaching some success, I still fear rejection.

- I often feel like I have no idea what I'm doing.

- I think more than I want to about other people's opinion of me.

- Despite all these things, I can overcome my fears, self-doubt, envy, burnout, and procrastination to work on being the writer I want to be.

Another thing I've learned after meeting dozens and dozens of other artists is that these thoughts and feelings are very common. It doesn't matter if a person has won awards, made Hollywood movies with multimillion-dollar budgets, had a best seller, or received thousands of five-star reviews on Amazon. There's something about creative work that can make you feel exposed and vulnerable. No matter how much experience or talent you might have, you can still feel uncertain. You can still lie awake and wonder, *Am I okay?* You can still feel embarrassment or even shame that you even *tried* to make something.

I don't know exactly why this is, but it is. And if you feel any of the things in my list, you are far from alone, and experiencing these fears does not mean you aren't or can't be creative.

That's what this book is about: the practical and emotional speed bumps and challenges I've experienced and have learned to work with and through, and my hope is that I can share that experience with you. I hope I can be a friend or sort of a big sister in these pages to encourage you in whatever you're doing and to offer advice and company along the way.

Though a lot of what I've written in this book is meant to apply to all sorts of creative endeavors, writing fiction is the thing I know the most about. Therefore, when I use examples from my own life and experience with the creative process, they will be about writing. But you can usually apply them to any kind of creative project you're doing because this book is less about what kind of art and how much of it we produce, and more about what's inside of us that can hinder our courage and steal away the joy of creating—which is not only an ability we all have but an essential part of being human.

## HOW TO USE THIS BOOK

This book is written both in a kind of order and in a loose shape. Therefore, if you read it *in order* (especially the first time through), it will probably make more sense. That said, you don't *have* to read it in order. No one is watching, grading, or judging you, so skip around if you want!

# Why We Become Afraid

To begin, let's break down the words in the title of this book.

*Courageous. Creativity.*

The word *courageous* means "brave, bold, daring." It also implies that there's something to be afraid of and that, in the face of that thing, we need courage.

How about the word *creativity*? Imagination, inventiveness, originality, resourcefulness, thinking outside the box, problem-solving—those are things that can be encompassed by *creativity*. What about the word *creative* as a way to describe people, like when we say, "Sara is so creative" or "I am not creative"? How have you heard it used? What is *creative* about?

- Being good at writing or drawing?

- Having a vivid imagination?

- Getting A's on your creative writing assignments or in art class?

- Winning a prize for a poem or a song you wrote?

- Having what people call "talent"?

- The opposite of the word *athletic*?

Or sometimes, does "You're so creative" mean something else altogether? Maybe sometimes it's what people say when they really *mean*:

- "You're lying."

- "You made that up."

- "Nice try."

- "Weird!"

- "You did it wrong."

The word means a lot of different things both to people who say it and to people who hear it.

It can be a compliment or a masked insult. An identity or a label. An accomplishment or a failure.

My take is that creativity is both so much more common and so much more mysterious than any of our definitions can capture. Think about little kids. Put just about any little kid in a room with some art supplies, some musical instruments, and room to play, and that kid will create. A scribble, a sound, a movement. Even babies who aren't walking yet, if given a couple of containers to keep them busy, will delight in realizing they can create a noise if they bash the two containers together.

As kids get older, you can ask them to imagine what's behind a closed door or inside a box, and that kid will create a story.

They make up songs, they make up words, they make up elaborate explanations for why the world is the way it is, they want to play with ingredients in the kitchen and make something. Sure, some of that is imitation of the adults and older kids around them or a response to being encouraged to create, but the bottom line is this:

- No matter where you were born, when you were born, or how you were born—you were born creative.

- No matter what language you speak or what clothes you wear or how much money you have, no matter whether you live in a house or an apartment or a car or a shelter, no matter whether you live in a big city or in the middle of a cornfield or in a suburb—you are creative.

- No matter whether you like sports, science, math, or reading, or don't think you're good at any of those things—you are creative.

- No matter the size or shape of your body, no matter the status of your physical or mental health, no matter the color of your skin or eyes or hair—you are creative.

We all use our creativity day in and day out, even if we don't think of what we're doing as "creative." For example, almost every day we will all use our creativity to do things like:

- solve a problem.

- make lunch.

- pick out what to wear.

- plan a birthday party.

- play with siblings or buddies.

- write notes or texts to friends in school.

- post to social media.

- complete homework.

- hum or whistle around the house.

So if we all have this thing inside us, and we use it every day, why does creativity sometimes feel like something to fear? Why do we need courage to bring it out in the form of some kind of artistic project like writing a story or poem, drawing, painting, dancing, or playing music?

If it's something that came so naturally to us when we were little kids, why does it now often feel difficult, scary, embarrassing, or uncertain?

I think one of the main answers to that is that somewhere along the way, we started *evaluating* what we used to just do for fun. We started *judging* ourselves and others using words like *bad, okay, good, better, best, worst. Talented* and *untalented. Gifted* and *not gifted. Creative* and *uncreative.*

Maybe it starts with school—grades and report cards and comparing your drawings or stories or art projects to what the other kids are doing. Maybe you saw the expression on your teacher's face when she looked at your painting, and then you saw her expression when she looked at someone else's, and you felt you came up short.

Maybe it started with getting compared to a brother or sister who was declared to be "more" or "less" creative than you. "You're good at sports, but your sister is creative." Do you see how it is implied that you can't like or be good at both?

Maybe it started the first time someone laughed at something you did. You felt hurt or embarrassed and decided never to put yourself out there again.

Maybe it started the first time you competed for a prize with a poem you had written, and someone else won instead. Or you got the prize and then you thought everything you did afterward also had to be good enough to get a prize.

Maybe it started when a parent or teacher said to you, "Some people are just more creative than others," and it was obvious that you were one of the "others."

Maybe it started with puberty, a time when we can be so overwhelmed with worries about whether we're okay, whether we're "normal," what other people think of us, and whether we fit in that even walking out the door to go to school feels like a risk—let alone sharing a story we wrote.

It's probably all or many of these things in some combination. We're always getting messages, directly and indirectly, from the world around us about how we're supposed to be, what things are okay to feel proud of versus what we should be ashamed of. We learn to see the world as divided into winners and losers, good and bad. We learn to categorize and label people: athletes, brains, troublemakers, rule-followers. We find the categories that seem to fit us—or someone else finds them and puts us in them before we've had a chance to decide for ourselves—and we stay there. If we poke a toe over the line into a different category, people sometimes get uncomfortable and try to put us back where we were.

To add to all of that, we live in a world where the words and pictures we dare to put out there on social media can be given an immediate thumbs up or heart or smile or frown with one click or tap. We're encouraged by corporations to rate everything we watch, read, and listen to on the same five-star scale. Movies, music, TV shows, videos, and books are always in competition for views and ratings and awards. Which makes us nervous when we think about creating our own thing because what if no one likes it? What if the world decides we're worth two stars out of five?

We label people as "artsy" and think it has to mean something specific and externally recognizable (like having multicolored hair, or walking around carrying your trumpet, or reciting poetry at a coffee shop). And if we have some secret suspicion that we might be "artsy" too, but no one else thinks so, it can feel like it takes an act of courage to say, "I made something," or "I *want* to make something," even to ourselves.

Sometimes, all we need to get us started is permission. That can be a harder thing to give ourselves than you might think. It was definitely hard for me.

# My Story

The family I grew up in had a lot of problems and challenges. Good qualities too, but the problems kind of got most of the energy and attention. My dad was an alcoholic, and that affected just about everything else for me, my mom, and my sister. His drinking problems led to money problems, and money problems created a lot of stress. Mental and emotional health problems also go hand-in-hand with drinking problems, and my parents didn't really know how to be honest about what they were feeling and experiencing, so my sister and I didn't learn that either.

You could say we mostly lived in survival mode—getting through each day to make it to the next, and not having a lot of energy, time, or skills to think much about the future.

Because of these things, I did not learn how to "dream big" about my own future. In fact, I don't remember any conversations with my parents about what I might like to do when I grew up, what kind of job I might want to have, what I might want to study in college, or what I was *really* interested in (as opposed to what I thought I *should* be interested in).

I didn't get messages that told me I was capable of doing hard things, or that it was okay to try things and fail at them, and those skills were not modeled by the adults closest to me. It's not like anyone told me I *wasn't* capable or *shouldn't* dream, but the absence of those conversations sent a silent message that I didn't even know I was getting.

It's amazing how strong and clear silent messages can be! When we're kids, we're really good at sensing the unspoken rules about what is okay and not okay to say and do in our families. We internalize these rules—that is, they become a deeply rooted part of us whether or not we meant to let them do that, whether or not we even understood them.

Some of the unspoken rules I absorbed from the unhealthy dynamics in my family were:

- Don't expect too much, and if you do have any dreams or expectations, don't talk about them.

- Don't talk about uncomfortable feelings like sadness, anger, or fear.

- Don't want too much because you probably won't get it—survival mode!

- Don't depend on people to be there for you.

- Stay small and out of the way, and keep your needs manageable.

- Don't think too highly of yourself—that's vain.

- Don't put yourself out there—you might fail!

There were other lessons and rules too, and in some ways I am still realizing the impact these silent messages had on me.

One thing I understand now as an adult was that my father was a "failed" artist himself. He studied music in college, got his PhD in music, taught music, did vocal performance, and even conducted an orchestra. My mother too had always been a musician, and studied music at the same college as my father, though I don't think her expectations for herself were as high as my father's were for himself.

Because of his alcoholism, my father kept losing jobs and opportunities in the creative fields he wanted to work in, and he carried a lot of shame about that.

Of course, I didn't know all this when I was a child, but now I can see how my dad's struggles to be courageously creative were part of those silent messages transmitted to me and my sister.

I learned not to expect too much, but I did not learn not to want and need. It is not "too much" to want and need love, affection, security, acceptance, encouragement, help, and guidance. In fact, in a healthy family system these are perfectly reasonable expectations.

As we grow up, we also want some way to use our talents, skills, imaginations, and interests to express who we are or who we might be. This desire too is completely natural and healthy.

I was in my mid-teens when I started thinking seriously that I might want to be a writer.

But I kept it a secret.

If I didn't tell anyone what I wanted, then no one could shoot down my dream. No one could tell me, "Well, that probably won't happen." Or "What makes you think *you* can do that?" Also, if I secretly tried and then felt like I failed, I wouldn't have to deal with anyone asking, "Didn't you want to be a writer or something? What happened with that?"

If I didn't tell anyone, I wouldn't be in a competition with anyone where I could win or lose. I couldn't be compared to others, and I couldn't be criticized.

In my late teens, I started quietly attempting to put the stories in my imagination into words on paper. I had the first few pages of many stories, but I didn't know how to stick with them. The problem with not telling anyone what you're trying is that it means you can't ask anyone for help.

Another part of my secrecy was the strange shame I felt about wanting to write, wanting to be a writer. It must have been related to shame I absorbed from my unhealthy family system.

I even felt a bit like I was doing something wrong because no one had given me "permission." I'd never taken a class or a workshop, or met an author. As far as I knew, "authors" were fancy people in New York City who had some kind of special knowledge. Was it okay for me—a kid from a challenging background way out on the West Coast—to even try?

When I went to college, I registered as an English major. Not because I really wanted to be an English major. At the same time, no one told me I *had* to be an English major. It just seemed like one of those choices I was supposed to make. After all, I got good grades in English in high school, my older sister was an English major, we were all readers in our family . . . so studying English felt safe. Meanwhile, secretly (so secretly that I barely knew it myself), I wanted to study theater arts, film, or creative writing. What was I going to do with an English degree? Be a teacher? Teaching is great and important, but it wasn't what I wanted.

The fact that I didn't want to be an English major soon expressed itself in my not doing my homework. My grades were not good. My papers were not good. I hated it.

I changed my major to something just as safe but with more job options at the end of it. I didn't love that either, but I did okay.

Note: I am *not* saying you have to study something commonly understood as "creative" in college to be on a creative path. And you can definitely be interested in more than one thing. You can go to college and study science and still be an artist. You can study economics and be a painter. You can not go to college at all and be a self-learner. You don't even have to know what you want at eighteen or twenty-two or thirty. This story is simply to demonstrate how disconnected I was from my true self and why my creativity required courage.

I was so, so, so, *so very* afraid to dare to say to myself or anyone else what I wanted, because no one had taught me that it was allowed.

When I reached my mid-twenties, I started letting a few people in on my secret—that I thought I might kinda, sorta, maybe want to try writing something. I was super casual about it. *No big deal, I might try writing, whatever.* Then I would change the subject.

It took a while for me to get comfortable telling more people, to feel I "deserved" to be in a writing group, to start putting some of my words out there and submitting my writing for possible publication. I spent more time reading and learning about how to write, and about how the business of publishing works. I dedicated more hours to working on my stories.

Those first tentative steps of telling a few safe people what I wanted and hoped for, and spending time on what I wanted and hoped for, were some kind of internal signal: I was giving myself permission. I was starting to be courageous in my desire to make creativity a more intentional part of my life.

Maybe you don't have the problems I had (and sometimes still have) with expressing your creative goals and dreams. Maybe you have a family like mine but you came out with a different set of beliefs than I did, or maybe you have a family totally different from mine but you still somehow wound up with a lot of the same fears and concerns that I had. These fears and concerns can come from being in a family that values high achievement, being "perfect," being noticed, or being "important" in certain ways that society rewards.

Maybe you are totally comfortable talking about wanting to write (or paint or make movies or dance or sing or act). Maybe you are all good with dreaming big! Which is awesome.

But if not . . .

Now is the time to give yourself permission to create.

Right now.

If it's helpful to hear: *I give you permission to give yourself permission.*

No matter how "good" or "talented" you think you are or are not, no matter where you live, no matter where you come from, no matter what your parents do, no matter whether anyone has ever encouraged your creativity, no matter what: *you have permission.* As I've said and will keep saying, creating is a fundamental part of human nature! And if you are reading this, you are a human.

PERMISSION GRANTED, HUMAN Go forth and Make!

# P.S. Some Thoughts about Capitalism;
## or,
# "For Fun" vs. "For Money"

Does being creative count if you can't turn what you make into a career, money, fame, or a lifestyle brand?

Short answer: yes.

Long answer: the rest of this chapter, and in some ways, this book!

The concept of trading arts and crafts for other goods is far from new. Before there was money (and even after), there was bartering. We know of ancient trade routes from as early as 3,000 BCE, and many of the goods for trade were things like luxury textiles, jewelry, pots, and dishes.[1] A value was placed on well-made items that were pretty to look at and perhaps also useful.

Fast-forward to me at my desk here in the twenty-first century, and you find a world in which almost everything, including creative works, can be bought and sold. The amount of money a movie makes at the box office becomes part of its advertising.

---

1  Whipps, Heather. "How Ancient Trade Changed the World," LiveScience. https://www.livescience.com/4823-ancient-trade-changed-world.html

If a book sells enough to get on a best-seller list, that's a marketing point too, and we're supposed to believe that means it's better than books that don't make the list.

I've already talked about online likes and favorites and hearts and stars and views, but it's interesting to explore a bit further. Let's say you take a photograph of a tree. You really like this picture. It turned out exactly as you hoped it would and really captures the feeling you had when you first saw the tree. You post it to Instagram, and in a sense you are "paid" in likes. The more likes it gets, the more value you assign it in your mind. *Wow*, you think, *that was a really successful photograph*!

On the other hand, if it doesn't get very many or any likes, there's a good chance you will feel it failed. You wonder where you went wrong and why no one likes your tree picture.

Yet it's the exact same photograph it was when you took it and felt so satisfied.

We're trained by capitalism to want to treat creative projects (or anything we might make) as something to be turned into money ("monetized"), or into influence or fame or popularity. We're trained to think that the more money something makes or the more ad clicks it gets or the more social media interactions it receives, the more value it has. But the only thing capitalism can tell us is how much the *market* values what we've made. It can't tell us how valuable our creations *truly* are—or how valuable they are *to us*, how much joy they bring us in the making and sharing of them.

Why am I babbling on about this?

Because I believe that this strange, sometimes uncomfortable place where art and creativity meet capitalism has something to do with the issue of giving ourselves permission to create, and why that can require courage once we're past early childhood.

The message we get is that drawing, dance classes, playing an instrument, acting, and storytelling ("make believe" or "playing pretend") are all fine when you're a kid. We're even encouraged to do those things for fun. But then, as soon as we're old enough to "get serious" and start thinking about jobs and earning an income, picking a college major maybe, and thinking about what we'll do in the "real world," the question hanging over everything is: "But can you get paid for it?"

Is your art good enough to sell? Do you play well enough to get hired by a band? Can you get cast in a professional play? Would people buy your crafts at an arts fair booth? Is the thing you do good enough to trade for money, good enough to make into a career? Is it practical? Can it help you have financial stability?

If the answer to these things is *no* or *I don't know*, we are sort of trained to think, *Why do it, then? What if I'm never good enough to make money from it? Does that mean I shouldn't do it? Is it a waste of time?*

We may literally be told to "grow up." Or we may subtly understand we're supposed to get practical, that it's time to put away the paints and crayons and costumes.

In any case, most of us are so saturated in this kind of thinking from the world around us that it can be hard to identify it within ourselves and, most importantly, to question it.

We can practice questioning it by remembering that the things we make, post, and share have intrinsic value—even if that value doesn't translate into money or fame. The experience of making has intrinsic value. If you create and get something out of the act of doing it, or if the end result is satisfying to you, that's enough.

Personally, since I am right in the middle of that art-meets-commerce space as a published author, I have to remind myself of these things almost constantly. The temptation to judge and evaluate myself on sales and money (and likes and stars and followers) instead of based on the experience of what I'm doing and the quality of the end result is ever present. Remaining aware of and anchored to the intrinsic value of my work is vital yet challenging.

With all of that said, there's absolutely *nothing wrong* with wanting to be published, wanting to perform for an audience, wanting to make a creative passion into a job someday, wanting to be able to pay bills with your art. That is a completely worthy goal and a legitimate path to take. I would be a hypocrite if I said otherwise!

I am writing this book you have in your hands right now for

money. Yes, I love the topic and have a lot I want to say and share; I want to write the kind of book I wished I had twenty years ago. But I am also getting paid for it, and like all people, I need some source of income to pay for my food, clothing, shelter, and everything else.

I made it my goal twenty years ago to write for money, and I got lucky enough to see it happen. That's my reality, and I am very tangled up in the capitalism part of being a writer. I don't ever want to pretend that's not true. I never know if I can trust authors who say they'd keep writing even if it wasn't their job. How do they know?

Yet, as I said, I know there was a certain amount of luck involved in my being able to become a professional writer. It's not something fully in my or anyone's control. And I'd be lying if I said I wouldn't be sad if it hadn't worked out the way it did. Would I still be writing now? Would I still be trying to get published? I have no way of knowing that.

What I *do* know is that I would be doing something creative, because creativity matters to me and it always has. Before I was a writer, I played the clarinet and acted in community theater. When I couldn't get a part, I worked backstage. It never occurred to me to try to make either playing clarinet or acting something I could do for money, and I still loved the heck out of both of those things. Playing in an orchestra, singing in choir, and being part of a theater group all allowed me to spend time with other people who liked what I liked, and we could all feel the joy of making something together.

I also enjoy cooking, which feels creative to me. I enjoy taking pictures. I enjoy working on screenplays that I'll probably never finish, and I suspect I would keep on enjoying all those things even if I made my living working in an office rather than by writing.

Here's the bottom line of what I'm trying to say:

There is lots of intrinsic value in having creative pursuits for your own enjoyment, or for the social aspects of it, or for the experience, or for other non-marketplace reasons.

*And...*

Trying to break into the creative marketplace and maybe make art for a living is also a worthy goal and is not bad, shallow, or "selling out."

You might find yourself doing both; many artists do.

The important thing is to know the difference, and to not judge the intrinsic value of what you're doing based on external measures. Don't let your love of the picture of the tree, or your joy in taking it, get taken away by how many likes it gets or doesn't get.

Follow the path that gives you access to your own creativity, enables you to express yourself freely, and brings you lasting satisfaction.

Where does creativity start?

It starts with play.

Think back to when you were a little kid, a time when a lot of people were at their most freely creative. We didn't call it "being freely creative" back then, though. We just called it playing.

We start out life playing with sounds and movements, playing with words, playing with materials like paint and paper and fabric—exploring and interacting with the world around us. It's how we learn and discover, and is actually a really important part of physical and emotional development.

As we get older, we start playing with ideas. We have our jokes-and-riddles phase. Our magic-tricks phase. The phase when we make up elaborate stories to explain the world to ourselves and others, or to soothe our fears, or just to see how our parents react. We like to play dress-up and pretend to be other people or characters we've read about in books or seen in movies or on TV.

Play is deeply connected to the imagination, and in childhood our imaginations are encouraged and celebrated. We scribble some lines on the back of an envelope and our parents put it on the fridge. They sit through repeated tellings of our favorite jokes, and they laugh. They watch us dance around the living room in silly costumes, and they clap.

Then it seems like the season of sanctioned, celebrated free play comes to an end and our lives start to fill with homework, extracurricular activities like sports, and other responsibilities.

Play doesn't have to end, but after early childhood it requires more intention. Putting intention behind play is a big part of what this book is about. This section is about ways to get back into the habit of play and exploration (if you've lost it since getting older) or to make that habit more intentional.

Remember, creative play is not about being perfect. It's not even about being sort of good. It's about getting in touch with your imagination and discovering what might come out if you gave it time and space to roam. So if you're putting pressure on yourself to come up with a YouTube-ready song or a publishable story, take that pressure right off! You can always apply pressure again later if you really want to. But for now, let's play.

# Claim a Creative Space

When you were a little kid, did you have a place where you most liked to sit and draw?

Maybe you felt pulled to the kitchen table so you could be in the middle of a lot of activity, with your family walking in and out or even sitting with you to color or do crafts.

Or maybe you liked working in your room, where you could have some privacy and really get into your imagination without any interruptions. Was the yard your space? Being out in the air and sunshine, maybe with a family pet nearby?

It might have been something in between, some corner of a room or place in the house where you felt cozy and in your own space, but not lonely or separated from others. Maybe it was a mix of all those things, and your favorite space probably shifted as you got older and more independent.

For some of us, the space wasn't even in our own homes. When I was a kid, I didn't always feel relaxed or emotionally safe enough in my house to get into creativity. I liked it at my best friend Christine's house, because I always felt welcomed by her mom and she had tons of art supplies. I also really liked the public library (and taking long walks alone, which was a thing kids did in the 1970s!).

As I write this, I'm sitting at a table in a coworking space, which is kind of like a big shared office that you pay monthly rent to use. There usually aren't that many people here, so for me it's a nice atmosphere where I'm not alone but I'm also not feeling crowded. Sometimes I like working at coffee shops or libraries for the same reason. Other days, when I don't want to leave the safety and security of my own house, I sit at the dining room table, in front of a window. I also have a room in my house that's technically my "office"—it has my desk and shelves full of books. Even though I don't end up actually writing at that desk very much, I would call it my designated creative space. It's my desk, and no one else puts anything on it or sits at it, and it's where I can keep my laptop and notebooks and pens and reference books when I'm not using them. I'm lucky to have so many options!

I often observe other people out at libraries and coffee shops with a notebook, a computer, or a sketchpad. On nice days, I might see people drawing or writing at the park, or standing in front of an easel where they have a good view of a lake, a garden, a mountain.

What I like about being out in a public space is that I can observe people in the world around me. The more I observe about other humans, the better I am at writing about them. Or sometimes I'm not observing but I just want to soak up the energy of being out, to keep myself from feeling my world shrink down to only whatever I can see or hear through my screens.

There's no one right way to have a creative space and, like me, you might end up with several. But designating *somewhere* as a regular or favorite place to work on your creative projects can be a way to signal to yourself and to other people: "This is where I create." That's a good place to start when you're establishing a creative habit.

Claiming creative space can be broken down into two aspects: the physical space and the mental space.

## A PHYSICAL PLACE

As you play and experiment with designating a space to do your writing, drawing, painting, dancing, music, or other creative endeavors, think about the following:

1. Your practical needs. The kind of space that works will of course partly depend on what you like to do. Writing and drawing can be done almost anywhere. Dancing needs more room. Things like painting or playing an instrument have different requirements. If you play piano, obviously you need to be wherever the piano is. If you play guitar, you can be more mobile. If you sew, you probably want a pretty permanent space where you can keep a sewing machine and all your fabrics and threads.

2. Your personal preferences. Do you like to curl up on the corner of the couch with your project, or spread out on the floor, or be alone in your room, or be with friends? Do you like it quiet, or do you like to listen to music or have activity around you? These things will affect what kind of space works for you.

3. Your reality. Maybe you share a room with a family member or members, move around a lot, or live in some other situation where you don't really have your own permanent space. Maybe for you, a creative space will be a special shoebox or backpack where you keep your art supplies or a notebook and whatever inspires you, like a favorite old toy, a picture that means something to you, a book you read again and again.

   Maybe there is nowhere in your house where you feel relaxed and safe, and your creative space will be at school or in a library or even at a relative's or friend's house where you do feel safe or can keep some supplies. (If this is you, I understand, and I'm so sorry. You have the right to take steps to create safe space for yourself and to express yourself creatively. If you can't figure out a way now, you will have a chance to do so in the future when you have more say about where and how you live.)

**"I THRIVE IN THE CHAOS OF AN ACTIVE ENVIRONMENT. COFFEE SHOPS, PARKS, EVEN MY DINING ROOM TABLE WITH MY KIDS AND DOG SWIRLING AROUND ME . . . THESE ARE MY FAVORITE WRITING SPOTS. I SETTLE INTO MY SEAT, PUT ON MY HEADPHONES, AND BLAST SOME DOOM METAL (DON'T JUDGE), CREATING A COCOON OF SOUND THAT KEEPS THE DISTRACTING SOUNDS AT BAY, WITHOUT LOSING THE ENERGY I GET FROM A ROOM FULL OF LIVING BEINGS. SOMETHING ABOUT WRITING WITH PEOPLE NEARBY KEEPS ME GROUNDED IN THE REAL WORLD. IT'S AS IF SOME OF THEIR HUMANNESS SEEPS INTO MY WORK, MAKING MY CHARACTERS JUST A LITTLE MORE REAL IN THE PROCESS. AT LEAST I LIKE TO THINK SO."**

*—SCOTT TEEMS, WRITER-DIRECTOR*

Taking into account these three factors—your practical needs, personal preferences, and reality—explore your options. If you have your own room, maybe you can rearrange furniture to make a space for your projects and practice. There might be a corner in an attic or basement or garage you can claim as your own. Maybe a family member or friend would be willing to help you transform it if it needs some TLC. Maybe you're perfectly happy doing your projects at the kitchen table! Try different places and spaces, and learn what you like.

Making a creative space can be a creative project in itself!

## A STATE OF MIND

Ultimately, the most important creative space you have is in your mind.

Whatever constraints there are on physical space in your life, remember this: your mind is free, and within it is a vast landscape. What you build and let grow there is yours. It can't be taken away if your family moves or you lose your home, if you have to share your room with others, if your art supplies get stolen, if your school burns down, or if your computer crashes.

You can build a permanent space for creativity within yourself that can't be destroyed.

It can, however, be crowded out and neglected. Our brains are taking in and sorting through millions of little pieces of information every day. It gets very full in there! And the older you get and the more complicated life becomes, the more things fill your mental space—more to do, more to worry about, more to learn. We meet more people, get more homework, have more complicated friendships. As we move into high school,

**"IN THE DEPTH OF WINTER, I FINALLY LEARNED THAT WITHIN ME THERE LAY AN INVINCIBLE SUMMER."**

*—ALBERT CAMUS, AUTHOR AND PHILOSOPHER*

we might have jobs, romantic interests, family responsibilities.

Then there might be college and then adult life. Which has a way of filling in every available space in your mind, if you let it.

But you don't have to let it.

Part—a *big* part—of having a creative practice that can serve you for life is protecting that space within yourself where your imagination can roam, you can ponder ideas, ask yourself questions, build images, notice the world.

Start building that place inside you now and practice using it and protecting it, and it will always be there for you. Even if it gets crowded by life sometimes or you neglect it for a while and forget it's there, all you have to do is clear out the junk and turn on the light and it will be waiting for you.

Let's talk about how we use creative play to build that space and keep it warm and well lit!

# Claim Your Time:
# Creativity Appointments

Closely related to space is time.

We can work on our physical space for creativity, but it's pointless if we don't make time to use it. And when it comes to mental space, time is the very tool that builds and maintains it.

One of my favorite books about writing is *Becoming a Writer* by Dorothea Brande. It was written way back in 1934. I first read it myself about twenty years ago, and I still look at it at least once a year. The foundation of Brande's advice on becoming a writer is to make appointments with yourself to write on a schedule. She called it a "debt of honor" to keep an appointment with yourself. "You have decided to write at four o'clock, and at four o'clock write you must! No excuses can be given."[2]

A lot of other writers and artists have echoed this basic advice: intentionally claiming time for your creative practice is the best way to make it happen. Time is a limited resource, and it gets gobbled up quickly by school, work, homework, family obligations, extracurricular activities, chores—not to mention sleep! If you happen to have free time, it can easily get lost to staring into a smartphone or a computer screen. Time slips through our fingers before we even realize we had a chance to catch it.

2  Dorothea Brande, Becoming a Writer, (New York: Macmillan, 1996), 77.

Some people have no trouble at all keeping up a creative habit without having to think about it. I know one or two of them. Maybe that describes you! But the majority of even the most creatively driven and talented people I know have to put some kind of planning and intention into making writing, music, dance, drawing—whatever their thing is—a regular priority that allows them enough time to grow and develop their interests, practice their skills, and explore processes and techniques.

What about inspiration? What about just writing or drawing when you *feel* like it? When you're in the *mood*? When you're putting away the dishes and you get a great idea for a story?

Yes, moments of inspiration are also good times to write or create. There's absolutely nothing wrong with creating when you feel inspired. I definitely do!

But I've had a few problems with the *writing mood*. One is that it's **very unreliable**. I can go weeks without the mood showing up, taking me by the hand, and pulling me to my desk to get words down. The other thing about the *writing mood* is that it can be **very quiet**. Inspiration is more likely to speak in a whisper than a shout. Unless I intentionally make the time to listen for it, it gets drowned out by the general noise of life and schedules, which is why I put it in my schedule. Lastly, the *writing mood* is also **very vulnerable to resistance**, a thing we'll talk about a lot more.

Inspiration has its place, but I—and many, many other artists—find it's more likely to show up if we clear space and time for it first.

Dorothea Brande says that if you make an appointment with yourself for creativity and the time comes when you've planned to do it (say, four o'clock), you must drop everything and *do* it, no matter what, to pay that "debt of honor." Now, I am nowhere near that strict. That kind of strictness doesn't work for me—it only makes me want to rebel! But the underlying point is about intention. If you want to cultivate your creative practice, you have to actually *intend* to do it and give some thought about how and when it will happen. Rarely does it magically fall into your lap.

With all that in mind, think about your daily life, schedule, and responsibilities. When could you fit in a creativity appointment?

It doesn't have to be long. Even twenty or thirty minutes is a lot of time when you aren't also checking your phone or getting otherwise interrupted.

## "TIME IS THE COIN OF YOUR LIFE. IT IS THE ONLY COIN YOU HAVE, AND ONLY YOU CAN DETERMINE HOW IT WILL BE SPENT."
### —CARL SANDBURG, WRITER

# "YOU CAN'T USE UP CREATIVITY. THE MORE YOU USE, THE MORE YOU HAVE."
### –MAYA ANGELOU, WRITER

Is there a little pocket of time right after dinner? Or maybe between school and dinner? Personally, I don't like getting up early in the morning (okay, I hate it), but plenty of creative people I know love that early-morning time for creativity appointments.

A creativity appointment doesn't need to happen every day. Maybe you schedule twenty minutes on Tuesday afternoons and an hour on Saturday mornings. Maybe you have no time during the week, but Sunday afternoons are totally free.

It doesn't matter when or how long it is; the important thing is to think about it, schedule a time, and stick to it the best you can. If you're not in a creative habit now, it will probably take some trial and error to find a length of time and the days that feel best.

It's possible the idea of creativity appointments feels like a rule, and maybe rules around creativity stress you out. Maybe writing "play time" on a calendar or scheduling a reminder on your phone sounds too much like an assignment, and your inner rebel says *no*. Trust me, I get it. My inner rebel is a force I always have to reckon with. If that's you too, it's going to be okay.

You can learn to work *with* that aspect of yourself instead of against it by thinking of things like creativity appointments and the suggestions that follow as tools. You can pick up any of these tools and try them, and you can put them down again whenever you want. *Tools, not rules!*

Now, whether you choose your creative play time through making an appointment or you do it in a more spontaneous way, the question is: What do you *do* with that time?

You might already have a very clear idea of exactly what you want to make and play with, but if you don't—if you are in between ideas, or if you have *no* idea what you want to do or how to get started—these next sections are here to help.

# Freewriting: Not Just for Writers!

*Freewriting* might be a totally new word or idea to you, but chances are you've done it in school at some point. It's something you can use whether you're a writer or a musician or a visual artist, or if you have some other kind of non-writing creative focus.

Let's say you've made your appointment or spontaneously found some creative play time. You're in your spot and you're ready to go. And you think to yourself, "Now . . . play!"

And you sit there.

Your inner voice says, "Aaaaand PLAY! Write something! Draw something! Make something! You said you were going to *be creative!*"

You freeze.

"Wow, you can't even, like, *be creative* for five minutes. What's the matter with you? I SAID PLAYYYYY!"

Okay, maybe my inner voice is meaner than yours, but maybe this sounds familiar to you. You can see how quickly something that's supposed to be fun can turn into one more thing you feel like you're *supposed* to do and that you could fail at. Creativity can quickly go from fun idea to seemingly impossible nightmare.

This is when freewriting can save the day.

Freewriting is a specific way of using the act of writing to get past your critical-thinking processes—the unhelpful chatter in your head that says mean or anxious stuff like:

You get the idea. It's very easy for us to get frozen or caught in a thought loop that keeps us from ever getting anything started. Freewriting can help get you out of that loop. Here's one way to do it:

1. Set a timer for five minutes.

2. Put a pen or pencil to paper.*

3. Write.

4. Do not stop until the timer goes off. Keep your hand moving.

For the writing itself, you can start with anything that's in your mind. Start by putting your doubts into words. You can literally write about how this is hard and dumb and you should be cleaning the cat box. You can write about what you're wearing, what you want to do later, and what's going on at school. Or what you'd do if you won a million dollars or had to move to another country.

Do not correct yourself! Do not worry about your grammar or spelling or handwriting!

Basically, you want to spill your messy thoughts onto the paper. You want to try to empty the junk in your brain that's intruding on your creativity appointment. Shake the sand out of the shoes of your mind? I think you know what I'm getting at.

You might find that after a minute or two of this, you've successfully raked up the dead leaves of thoughts and uncovered

---

*You can also do this on a computer, but if you are able to write by hand on paper, try it! Handwriting is a slightly different cognitive process than typing and can tap into other parts of your brain.

the good dirt, and you realize you *do* actually have some creative ideas in there that you want to play with.

What might this look like? Maybe you're dumping out the contents of your anxious mind and you start writing about something that happened at school that made you feel embarrassed or uncomfortable. You want to write it as a story—maybe to explore why it made you feel that way, or to give the incident a better ending.

Or in the process of writing something like, *I am really bad at guitar and I only know three chords and my fingers won't reach all the strings*, you decide to put down your pen and pick up your guitar to prove to yourself how your fingers won't reach, then you work on playing the three chords you do know, and pretty soon you find you've been practicing for twenty minutes.

On the other hand, you might write for the whole five minutes and still feel kind of blah about the whole endeavor. It's not a magic formula that works for everyone. That's okay! You might start by freewriting, realize you *hate* freewriting, and decide you'd rather just do the thing you sat down to do in the first place, or that it's time to go ahead and clean that cat box.

The important thing is you showed up.

Keep showing up for yourself with good intentions, keep giving yourself permission, keep trying the tricks and tools in this book to shake stuff loose and clear space in your mind, and you will make forward movement.

# Brainstorming

I love the word *brainstorm*. A storm in your brain! A rush of activity and excitement! Thunder and lightning and rain! High winds! It's not tidy, but the chaos itself can reveal thoughts and ideas you didn't know were there. Brainstorming is another great thing to do during a creativity appointment.

Unlike freewriting, which I think of as a general dump of intrusive thoughts or a way to get your mind-body connection going, brainstorming is more specific to the actual creative ideas you have.

*Like* with freewriting, it's important not to criticize, analyze, or correct what comes out. You're not trying to make a masterpiece here; you just want to get down a lot of ideas to weed through and choose from later.

There are a lot of different ways to brainstorm. I personally am a fan of doing it on paper because, as I mentioned before, there is some science about how writing by hand helps you think more deeply and remember more. But you can also do this on a computer or a tablet or even a smartphone.

Let's say your creative idea is: "Make a five-minute movie about my dog."

You could start by making a list of ideas for the story of the movie; for example:

- day in the life of Spot—normal day
- Spot waking me up in the morning
- me taking Spot for first walk
- breakfast with Spot
- Spot greets me after school
- walk number two
- Spot naps
- dinner
- playing with toys
- saying goodnight

Then you could make another list about the style of the movie:

- black-and-white, like an old silent movie?
- or add music and edit the movie to the length of the song
- make it a comedy—put in a laugh track like a '90s sitcom

- make it more like a superhero movie with special effects—maybe could make a cape for Spot

You can also try different kinds of visual representations of your idea.

If painting or drawing is your thing, take a lesson from the masters and spend your creativity appointment doing "studies." According to Wikipedia, a study is a "drawing, sketch or painting done in preparation for a finished piece, or as visual notes."

For example, you might be familiar with the famous Edward Hopper painting *Nighthawks*, which he finished in 1942. It's a look in through a diner window at night. The diner appears to be on a deserted corner of a city block, and we see four people inside: three customers at the counter and one employee behind it. Two men are in business suits, there's a woman in a red dress, and the guy behind the counter wears an all-white outfit like diner workers did in the old days.

The painting is quite simple and uncluttered. That was Hopper's style. But there are a few small details in addition to the

**"I FIND FREEDOM IN NONSENSE— MY SONGS USUALLY BEGIN WITH GIBBERISH LYRICS TO ESTABLISH A MELODY BEFORE I EVENTUALLY FORCE THEM INTO SOMETHING RESEMBLING SENTENCES." —ANDREW REASE SHAW, SONGWRITER AND FILM COMPOSER**

people: the counter has a set of salt and pepper shakers on it, a napkin dispenser, a sugar shaker, mugs of coffee.

When I went to a Hopper exhibit at a museum some years ago and saw *Nighthawks* and Hopper's other work in person, I decided to buy a book about the artist. The book is *full* of his studies, and what stood out to me the most were the pages of little sketches of salt shakers.

Now, I don't know what Hopper's process was exactly, but I do know he did not sit down one day in front of a blank canvas and say, "I will now paint an epic piece that will become my signature work that people still be talking about and paying to see in museums in eighty years."

I imagine he had the image in his mind of a city diner late at night. That he wanted to capture the quiet of it, the way that a few people sitting at a counter at midnight can look lonely but also inviting, that he had seen something like that on his walks around the city and it struck him in some way that he wanted to capture in a painting.

I imagine how he started with his sketchbook and these small studies of salt shakers. How they warmed up his hands, helped him sink into his vision, helped him refine his idea of what this diner would look like when it was finished.

It's a more advanced kind of brainstorming done by someone who was already a skilled artist, but the concept is the same: that virtually no artist or writer just sits down and "paints a masterpiece" or "writes a novel."

All big creative works are done one stage at a time, one step at a time.

They start with scraps and lists and lines, word association and imagination, free thinking and free writing and free drawing. Putting a lot down onto paper or screen and not worrying about which of your ideas are better than others or if any of them are perfect.

We sketch a scene. Plunk out the beginnings of a melody. Write a sentence. Blend a color. Try a stitch.

These are the first small steps of developing a creative habit and, when you're ready, a creative project.

# Building an Attention Collection

There are things in life we clearly understand as resources. Money, for example. That's a resource, and it is limited—meaning there's not an unending supply of it (for most people). Time is another limited resource. Nothing will change the fact that there are twenty-four hours in a day, and generally, we use about a third of that for sleeping and another third of it for working and/or going to school. Just as some people have more money to spend than others, some people have more free time in a day. But essentially, we all work within those rough limits. And we're probably all familiar with the concept of a budget for managing money and have used things like calendars and timers for keeping track of time and for scheduling appointments (like creativity appointments!).

But what about our attention? Attention is not only the *time* we spend noticing particular aspects of people, places, and things, but also the amount of *focus* we give those things. For example, you could spend an hour at a park and not pay any attention to the park itself if you're absorbed in your phone or in a conversation with someone. You can sit through a class at school and leave realizing you didn't hear anything, because you were worried about something that had nothing to do with class.

# "TO PAY ATTENTION, THIS IS OUR ENDLESS AND PROPER WORK."
## –MARY OLIVER, POET

Some philosophers have said that attention is love. Some have said that we *are* what we pay attention to. You can agree or disagree with those statements, but I do think we can at least say this for certain: What we pay attention to has a significant impact on how we experience life.

You've probably noticed some version of the following:

- When you pay a lot of attention to bad news, you feel anxious and depressed.

- When you pay a lot of attention to good news, you feel hopeful.

- If you pay a lot of attention to your pets, you feel a bond with them.

- If you pay a lot of attention to social media, you might feel like you're not cute enough or clever enough or some other kind of not enough.

- You pay a lot of attention to your friends and you wind up knowing what's going on in their lives, and are therefore better at supporting them.

- You pay a lot of attention to knowing every detail of the Marvel Universe, and that makes you love it more than ever.

- You pay a lot of attention to what you think and feel, which helps you really start to know yourself and get good at knowing what makes you happy or sad or angry, and what kind of people you like to have around.

The point is, attention is powerful!

What we pay attention to can shape and change our moods, opinions, beliefs, likes, dislikes, and plans. And—like time and money—our attention is a limited resource. We can't pay attention to *everything*. To an extent, we get to choose what we give that resource to.

Writer David Dark uses the phrase "attention collection" to talk about this idea. I really love that phrase because it makes something abstract feel a little more concrete. I can imagine the things I pay attention to as if they are shells I'm picking up on the beach and putting into a basket. The basket gets heavier as I go. I can't just throw every single shell in there and still enjoy having them.

David Dark suggests that what we pay attention to makes up our "inner creative core."[3] What we put into that attention collection— what we carry in our thoughts and imagination, what we love and hate and fear and celebrate, what we're curious about and what we're afraid of—is all going to come out in what we create.

What's in your attention collection right now? Maybe you're not sure yet. Maybe you've never thought about it that way. That's okay. I can tell you some things that I know are in mine. This is all stuff I've paid extra attention to over my lifetime because of my own interests and fears and experiences:

- Fall weather
- How it feels to be left out

3 *David Dark*, Life's Too Short to Pretend You're Not Religious *(Downer's Grove: IVP, 2016), 66.*

- Cello music

- The memory of my parents' divorce

- All the different kinds of bubbly water there are

- Old movies from the 1940s that star the actress Bette Davis

- The fear of spiders and of going to parties

- The dancing scenes from the movie *Singin' in the Rain*

- The feeling of a cool breeze through a window and how I love it when the curtains blow around

- A hatred of the sound of leaf blowers

This is just a tiny sample. Does it seem like a strange list? Maybe it is. Maybe everyone's personal attention collection seems a little strange to someone else.

I do know that all of these things have come out in my writing in one way or another. It could be in the form of a character who also hates spiders and loves bubbly water. Sometimes it's more like trying to make someone reading my books feel the way I feel when I watch *Singin' in the Rain,* or trying to transmit through a character how it felt for me when my father left, because maybe someone reading the book will also understand that feeling or because I want to be understood.

Sometimes it comes out in using my knowledge to create an interesting setting for a book. For example, because I have paid so much attention to the sound leaves make when they scrape

# "PUT YOUR EAR DOWN CLOSE TO YOUR SOUL AND LISTEN HARD."
### –ANNE SEXTON, POET

across the street, and also the way a cellist bows her head over her instrument, I can pull those things out of my collection and use them in my stories to give depth of detail and character.

How do you build your own attention collection?

This is where an attention collection is pretty different from something like a seashell collection. If you're gathering seashells, you intentionally go out, you look, you bend down and pick up a shell, and you put it in your basket.

An attention collection is a mix of things you've already "collected" subconsciously just by being a human in the world. You've already got lots of stuff in there! Building an attention collection is almost more about *paying attention to what you pay attention to*.

You can start by making lists of things you know are extra-interesting to you, or that bring up extra-strong feelings. What do you love? What makes you afraid? What makes you feel joy? What sparks your curiosity? What things do you know a lot about?

From there, it's all about developing that attention to your attention. That is, when something comes into your field of awareness and is interesting enough or exciting enough or scary enough to you that it cuts through the noise of your brain in a particular way, make a note of it.

Doing this helps you be more aware of your thoughts, and can help you catch yourself when your attention is scattered in too many directions or, on the other hand, when it becomes hyper-focused on a single thing, not leaving any room to consider whether or not you want to be giving that thing so much attention.

A great tool for your attention collection is a paper notebook. I know I keep going on about the act of writing by hand, and here I'll mention it again: writing by hand, if you are able, will help you focus and pay even more attention to what you are paying attention to. A smallish notebook and pen or pencil that you can carry with you everywhere is good. Or you can fold an index card into a little square that fits in your pocket, keep a compact pen or a golf pencil with it, and always be ready to jot something down.

On the other hand, if you have a smartphone or device and like integrating it into your process, you can use a note-taking app. The fun thing about using a phone for your attention collection is that you can add images and voice recordings. If images are especially powerful for you, a private Pinterest board or something similar can be a great option. And if you lose or break the phone, your notes are likely still available somewhere in the cloud. The drawback of using a phone for this is that your attention is more likely to be interrupted by all the other things on the phone, and you might get caught up in sharing your thoughts or discoveries with others before you've had a chance to give them to yourself.

My personal method is a mix of old-school pen and paper and new-school apps and tech. I have numerous journals, I'm obsessed with pens, and I also love my smartphone.

And what goes into the collection? All kinds of stuff. In addition to the lists like "Things I know a lot about" and "Topics I want to explore," there are quotes and song lyrics; story ideas; facts I just learned that I might want to use in a story some day; fragments of writing, such as me describing how the last night of summer feels when there is that one cricket left still chirping all night; the titles of books I want to read or have read; the titles of books I want to write; things I want to know more about—anything that sparks something in me, anything I want to remember.

This concept of a notebook in which you put all sorts of bits of knowledge and interest goes way, way, way back. It is like Bible-times old! It was especially popular in the seventeenth century, when it was called "a commonplace book," which was essentially a notebook full of everything you wanted to remember that you knew and cared about: useful information, quotes, lists, etc.

Whether you call it an attention collection or a commonplace book or a diary or a journal or a notebook or something else, the idea is to learn more about yourself by understanding what captures your attention, making more intentional choices about what you pay attention to, and letting those things feed your life and creative work.

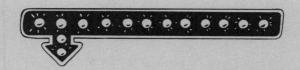

*By the way, I am not very organized! I have not streamlined this process or any of my creative processes at all. You should see all the notebooks I have in which the first dozen pages are used, then I misplaced it or got tired of that notebook and started a new one. I have thoughts written in illegible fragments on scraps of gum wrappers and a thousand emails to myself with the subject line "idea" (which, believe it or not, is not very helpful when you're searching your email). Do not think you have to have a perfect process to have a creative habit! There is no such thing as a perfect process or a right way to have a creative habit. It's very, very easy to get stuck in "Am I doing this right?" or "Is this the best way to do this?" and then never do anything at all. You can try one way of doing things, abandon it, try something else, invent new methods . . . it's all good! Tools, not rules!*

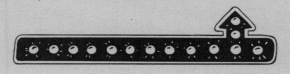

Once you've put in some time getting into a creative habit and have played with ideas and started to understand what's in your own attention collection, you might start to think more about a specific project that you want to do.

Maybe it's something long, like a book or a movie. Maybe it's something short: a video, a song, a series of poems, a quilt, or a costume.

Maybe you've had the idea for a long time, or maybe it's new.

The question is: How do you plan for actually *doing* it?

The question might also be: *Should* you even plan? Or should you . . . just *do* it?

There's no right answer. Plenty of artists take a "dive right in and see what happens" approach to their work, discovering as they go instead of thinking it all through from beginning to end. Then there are artists who are die-hard planners who never start anything without an outline or a schedule or a list of steps.

For all of us, regardless of instinct, planning can sometimes be very helpful in getting started on a bigger project and keeping from becoming overwhelmed by the details. This little section will touch on a few things to think about in the planning stages of a creative project.

# Intentions: What Do You Want to Do?

*Intention, goal, objective, aim*—these words all boil down to essentially the same thing: What is your desired result for your project? What do you want to make? What, specifically, do you want it to be when it's finished?

You probably have some kind of idea in your mind. You might even have the kind of imagination that can hold and sort out a *lot* of detail. Even if that's you, I highly recommend writing down a description of your project. This isn't something you have to share with anyone else. It doesn't have to be brilliant or well written. It's just a *description* of the thing, not the thing itself.

The purpose of this is twofold:

1. To know how much you know. You may know more about what you want to do than you think you know. The act of describing it helps bring out details, and you may be surprised at how many *more* specifics of the idea spill out when you describe it—especially for larger scale projects like books or plays or films. On the other hand, you may know *less* than you think you know. Your epic idea might need a lot more filling-out than you thought, and putting it all down can help you see where the holes are, what questions you still need to ask yourself, and what research you might still need to do.

**2.** To have a reference document you can go back to when you're in the middle of the project and you get overwhelmed and think: *What am I even doing and why am I doing it?* It's like building yourself a lighthouse. When things get foggy, you can return to what you wrote down to provide clarity and something to steer toward.

Here are some short examples of what this might look like:

*I want to write a seven-book series about life on the midwestern prairie in the nineteenth century. All about a pioneer girl and her family, their hardships, all the places they live and the people they know. I want it to feel adventurous but also cozy. I need to research covered wagons and prairie ecology. I am going to put in this notebook everything I know that will happen in the first three books but need to figure out the rest.*

Or:

*My goal is to write a Broadway rap musical about Alexander Hamilton, but first I just want to start with a few songs to see if it's actually a good idea. Getting a show on Broadway is hard! After I get a few songs written, maybe I can try it out at a smaller theater to get producers to invest in me so I can expand it into a Broadway-quality show. I know the basic outline of the plot because it's based on a biography I read—I just need to write it all down before I shape it into a play. I will need a really talented cast!*

Or:

*I want to record a concept album where all the songs are also videos, and it's as much a movie as it is an album. In between the songs, to join the videos together, I can have poetry and excerpts from my journal and stuff. I don't want to tell ANYONE I'm working on this other than the people I need to help me get it done! I'd rather it all be a surprise, and also that way, I can focus on my own vision and not let all those other opinions into my head.*

(In case you didn't figure it out, these examples are all real creative projects: the first one is Laura Ingalls Wilder's *Little House On the Prairie*, the second is Lin Manuel Miranda's *Hamilton*, and the last is Beyonce's *Lemonade*. I don't know if these three really came up with their ideas this way—but they could have!)

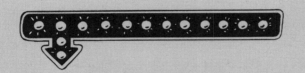

*If you've heard or read writers or filmmakers talking about their processes before, you might know what a "pitch" is. A pitch is a really short way of describing something you want or are going to do to the person or people who might enable you to do or finish or produce it. For example, a screenwriter might pitch an idea to a producer by saying, "My script will be about a kid who finds an alien in a cornfield, hides it in his room, and then has to*

*protect it from bad guys who want to steal it for experiments."*
*(This is the plot of the 1982 film* E.T.: The Extra-Terrestrial, *by the*
*way!) Professional authors like me will sometimes pitch ideas to*
*our agents or editors. "I was thinking my next book could be kind*
*of like* A Christmas Carol *but about Halloween and set in Iowa."*
*This short and catchy type of description is meant to influence*
*other people to get excited about what you're doing. When you're*
*writing your own intention just for you, it will probably have a lot*
*more detail, and you won't have to worry or think about anyone*
*else's opinion of it. But if it helps you focus your thoughts, you can*
*imagine how you'd do it if you only had a couple of minutes in an*
*elevator to describe it to someone else.*

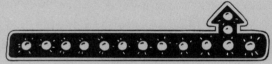

Once you've written out a description of your intent or
summary of the project to yourself, another type of goal you
might set is the amount of time you want to spend and/or
how much you want to get done each week on your project.
Some examples:

- Write 300 words a day, three days a week.

- Write for forty-five minutes on Tuesday and Saturday
  afternoons.

- Write three scenes of my script per week.

- Spend an hour practicing my song tomorrow.

- Try writing a poem a day for five days in a row.

As you can see, these are very specific and quantifiable, either in time spent or in work produced. (Writing lends itself to quantifiable goals because we end up with a number of words or pages or sentences. Other types of creative work might be more usefully measured in time—committing to a half hour a day, or five hours a week, or whatever time you have that works for you.)

I find specific, measurable goals extremely useful in planning my work and in making myself accountable to keeping up with my intentions so I can get to the end result I want. They also help me set limits so I don't get completely lost in my project and forget to look up from my computer, walk around, talk to people, and eat meals. They give me a sense of what is "enough" work—not too little and not too much.

Here's the thing about specific goals, though: If you are a perfectionist, not meeting them can create a whole bunch of anxiety, shame, guilt, and feelings of failure. If you fall behind, you might panic. If you were supposed to write 300 words today and you did zero, you tell yourself that tomorrow you'll do 600. And if you miss another day, that turns into 900 , then 1,200, and then pretty soon it's all too much and you get overwhelmed.

On the other hand, setting a reasonable goal and achieving it—no matter how small—can really be a boost to your confidence and sense of satisfaction. Say you set a small goal of 225 words a day, and

> **"A WRITER WORKS AT A PACE THAT WILL ALWAYS ALLOW FOR SUCCESS. FOR ME, THAT'S FIVE HUNDRED WORDS A DAY—AND THEN I STOP, NO MATTER HOW WELL THE HORSES ARE RUNNING. FIND THAT PACE AND STICK TO IT; ANYTHING MORE IS A SIREN'S CALL—AND YOU KNOW WHERE THAT LEADS."**
>
> **—GARY SCHMIDT, AUTHOR**

then you write 275. You're going to feel pretty happy with yourself! Then, if you regularly exceed your goal of 225, you realize you've built up the confidence and the muscle to up your goal to 300.

It's good to stretch yourself—the creative habit really is like a muscle. The more you use it, stretch it, and keep it warm, the stronger and more reliable it will be. But you don't start out lifting a 500-pound weight. To build your creative muscle and your self-confidence, it's better to set smaller goals that you can regularly achieve than to set bigger ones you are unlikely to meet.

Another important thing that happens when you set and achieve goals is that you are keeping a commitment you've made to yourself. You're sending a quiet but valuable message to yourself that your interests and dreams matter, and that you care about yourself and your goals. Showing up for yourself in a creative practice is a powerful kind of self-care.

If you find yourself easily stressed out and overwhelmed by goals that are too specific, you can be a little looser. Like:

- Write about 200–500 words a few days a week.
- Look for two free hours this week to work on my book.
- Take my script to a coffee shop on Saturday and write down any new ideas I got this week.

Goals and intentions are meant to help you develop your creative habits and get closer to a complete project. Try them out! If they aren't helpful and you discover you work better by jumping in and seeing what happens, that is 100% A-okay. Tools, not rules!

> **"I SCHEDULE MY WRITING JUST LIKE I SCHEDULE ANYTHING ELSE. IF I MAKE TIME AND SPACE FOR IT, A LITTLE EACH DAY, THEN THAT'S THE TIME I'M CREATIVE—AS OPPOSED TO WAITING FOR THE MUSE TO ARRIVE AND WHISK ME AWAY."**
> **–SARAH ENNI, WRITER AND PODCASTER**

# Deadlines: When Do You Want to Have It Done?

I don't know how deadlines work in every creative field, but I do know that they are a big part of life for professional writers. When we sign a book contract or get an assignment, part of the process is negotiating a deadline—the day on which you are expected to turn in a draft of your book or article. A contract often has a couple different deadlines, like a deadline for a first draft and a deadline for a final draft. The deadlines are related to the projected date of publication.

Personally, I have a love/hate relationship with deadlines.

Because I struggle a lot with perfectionism, fear, procrastination, and other stuff that can keep me from writing, I wonder sometimes if I'd ever finish anything without a deadline to help focus me. In that way, I love them. Or at least like them and am glad they're there.

At the same time, having a deadline reminds me of how I felt in school when I knew a big homework assignment was coming due. I'd look at my calendar and go, "Hmm, three weeks left." And not start it. "Okay, two weeks—let's go!" And not start it. "Oh, this is due next week?" And not start it. And I'd just make myself anxious by delaying until the last possible moment.

I don't know *why* I am like this, but I do this with book deadlines too. It's not quite the same as putting off homework, because you can't write a whole book the night before it's due. But something about the deadline being "out there somewhere" leads one part of my brain to say, "Plenty of time," and the other part of my brain to panic and stress. In those ways, I hate deadlines, though I suppose I can't blame the deadline so much as my own thought process *about* deadlines.

When you're working on a project for yourself, there's no real deadline in the sense of having consequences if you don't meet it. You're not going to get your book canceled or run out of money, the way professional writers might if they continually miss deadlines. Doing a creative project for yourself means no one but you really cares when you finish it or *if* you finish it at all. In a way, that's freeing. No one is watching. You can be messy and late and incomplete.

On the other hand, it can be very important for your own satisfaction, confidence, and sense of fulfillment to see projects through to the end. And if you are interested in creating professionally someday, it's crucial for you and everyone else involved to know that you can finish things.

So it might be a good idea to do some gentle practice with deadlines as a part of your goal-setting and planning process. If the word *deadline* has a little too much "dead" in it for you, you can call it a "target date" or use "finish by . . ." or something else. The idea is to set a general window of time by which you would like to complete your project.

Depending on the type and scope of the project, you might also set some in-between deadlines for various stages of the project. Sometimes these are called "milestones." For example, if you're making a five-minute video to ultimately post on a platform like YouTube or Vimeo, you might set different milestone deadlines like this:

| By [date]: | Task: |
|---|---|
| | make a list of shots |
| | confirm availability of cast and crew |
| | shoot all footage & capture all sound |
| | first edit |
| | final edit |
| | post |

If you're writing a book, it could be:

| By [date]: | Task: |
|---|---|
| | outline or summary of book |
| | first 50 pages |
| | finish rough draft |
| | finish final (?) draft |

You might be thinking to yourself: "But how do I know how long something takes if I've never done it before?" Great question! The answer is: You don't know! No one knows.

People who have written a few books or have made a few movies or have been doing music for years start to have a general idea of *approximately* how long something *usually* takes. But creative projects are not machinery. They don't just grind along at the same steady pace all the time. With writing, even if your daily word goal is steady—Gary Schmidt's 500 words, for example—you have no idea how long it will take you to do those 500 words. One day it could take half an hour. Another day it could take six hours. The work may come out in great gushing bursts followed by long stretches of barely a trickle. A short project could take longer than you ever imagined, and a long one could go unexpectedly fast.

Therefore—especially if you are new at what you're doing—deadlines will be educated guesses at best. If you're writing 500 words a few times a week, and you think your finished book might be 50,000 words, you can guess that a first draft might take about eight months to finish. If you're working on something like a short video or a song, your timeline might be more like a month or even less. You could do the first draft of a poem in one session.

But really, you can't ever be *certain*. The best you can do is:

- Calculate an educated guess or estimate.

- Adjust it as you go if you need to.

- Be gentle with yourself if you need more time!

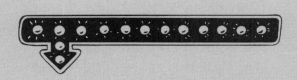

### WAIT, WHAT? SARA, DID YOU SAY EIGHT MONTHS?

*Yes, writing books might be the longest-term kind of long-term projects there are. Many people go faster than the example I gave; many go slower. But I'd say most writers I know think in terms of "about a year" for writing and rewriting a book. This is why I really enjoy the things that give me little bursts of creativity with immediate gratification, like doing an Instagram story or taking photos, writing little essays for my newsletter or online magazines, and working on short stories on the side. If you're doing a project with a big scope like a novel or movie, you might like to have some smaller things you also do so you can more often experience that satisfaction of finishing something.*

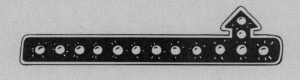

# Outlines?
# Yes/No/Maybe So

Speaking of novels and movies and longform projects like that, a part of the planning process might be a story outline, synopsis, or treatment. Maybe even storyboards or sketches.

You can find writers of all types who are passionately for or against outlining. It's almost like an identity for some writers: "plotter" (someone who plans it all out) or "pantser" (one who prefers to "fly by the seat of their pants").

Of course, that's a false dichotomy, because you can do a little of both on any given project. I think one reason many writers so strongly identify with one or the other has to do with knowing their emotions, how their imagination works best, and what their anxieties or fears are around getting a creative work done.

Some writers feel anxious if they don't have some kind of an outline. By writing themselves an outline first, they are almost giving themselves instructions on "how to write this book," and working from instructions can make the whole process much less scary or uncertain. It can prevent them from freezing up or procrastinating, because it reduces the fear of the unknown or the blank page. An outline can serve as a guide, a hand to hold, a continuation of that idea of building yourself a lighthouse when you start out so you'll know what to steer toward when you're lost.

Other writers feel anxious when they *do* have an outline. To them, it feels like a cage, like handcuffs. It takes some of the joy out of the creative process, and they would rather experience the thrill of discovering the story as they go. The blank page isn't scary to them—it's freedom! They worry that having an outline will make them blind to what *could* happen if they've already decided what *will* happen.

But like I said, I think it's a false dichotomy. It's not either-or. I think you can be a plotter *and* a pantser, have both direction *and* freedom. Here's how that looks in my own process:

I usually start by diving in. No outline—just an idea. Some combination of an image or a character or a situation. Maybe I just have the first sentence of a book in mind and I want to follow it and see where it takes me. This feels most like the play we talked about earlier in this book.

Then I get to a certain point with the story—maybe a couple of chapters, maybe fifty pages, maybe more—where I realize I have a vague idea of what's going to happen for the rest of the book and I want to write it down. There are certain scenes I know will take place but I'm not sure exactly where or when. I know there are conversations the characters will have at some point. I think I have an idea of how the book will end, or of a couple of possible endings.

That's when I write an outline, which for me is more like "This is probably, maybe, approximately what I think will happen for the rest of this book." It's just a probability, not a blood oath. It helps me shape the story and gives me some direction as the story gets more complicated, and if I change my mind or the story takes me somewhere else, that's fine! I can always rewrite the outline if I need to.

The important thing to remember is that an outline or a plan is supposed to be a helpful tool, not a pair of handcuffs. It is *extremely* likely—almost guaranteed—that as you get into the actual making of a longform project, it will change. You'll get new ideas about what you want it to be when it's finished and what it should contain. You'll realize you forgot something important or that you have a lot of stuff in there you don't need.

That is all totally normal, expected, and fine. You can change your outline as needed, make adjustments, or throw it away if it's no longer useful.

*Here are some broad definitions of different types of planning documents, and they will vary a lot from writer to writer and project to project. There are whole books and lots*

of websites out there that get into technical detail about how and why to use the various types of outlines, as well as where storyboards and character sketches might fit in. Some people get extremely specific in their outlines, perhaps following a template, formula, or common structure; others are not that precise.

**Outline:** A kind of written skeleton for what you plan to put in your book. People use all sorts of formats for this: a general sense of the story broken down into big chunks of beginning, middle, end; a list of chapters with a few lines or a couple of paragraphs about what will be in each one; a list of every single scene from start to finish. This is usually something authors use for their own reference in the process of writing the book.

**Synopsis:** Similar to an outline, but a little more formal and polished. Often this is what authors will show their agents or editors to communicate, "Here is the book I want to write; what do you think?" A finished synopsis will be maybe 7–20 pages describing the characters, the setting, what happens in the book, the emotional themes, the major plot points, and how it ends (if you know). Even if you're not working with an editor or agent, and not looking for one, writing a synopsis can be a helpful way to tell the story to yourself with as much polish and precision as you can.

**Treatment:** The word used in the movie, television, and screenwriting world to describe something that is sort of like a synopsis, though it might have some outline elements too. A treatment is a screenwriter basically communicating, "Here's how I see this movie." It might be 10–20 pages, depending on the story. If it's for a TV series, it will probably also have at least a sampling of what happens in each episode. It is mostly written in prose (regular sentences and paragraphs, not screenplay format, though it could include short scenes and sections of dialog written in script format).

Here are some search terms if you're interested in looking up more about outlines and outline-like documents:

- *Three-act structure*
- *"Save the cat"*
- *Book outline examples*
- *Novel synopsis examples*
- *How to write a synopsis for a novel*
- *How to write a book proposal*
- *How to write a movie treatment*
- *"TV series bible"*

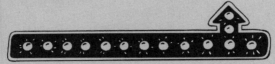

You've embraced creativity as your birthright! You've given yourself permission! You've played and plotted and planned and you've got a specific creative project in mind!

Now it's time to make the thing!

And if you've followed all the steps and been a good little trouper, making the thing will be so smooth and easy, right?

Wrong!

First of all, there is no such thing as following the steps. Remember, there aren't rules about creativity, just tools—concepts and methods and resources you can pick up and put down as needed and as you discover what works for you.

*Tools, not rules!* Chant that as much as you need to when you start worrying that you aren't doing it "right."

Second, creativity is not a straight path with a finish line. It is much more like a circle or a maze, or like a favorite hiking trail that looks a little different in every season and even a little different from day to day. In my experience, no two days of writing are alike. None of my books have followed the same process or taken the same amount of time as any other ones. I've been doing this for over twenty years and still have not reached a point where I feel anywhere near 100 percent confident that I know what I'm doing.

**"WHEN I FEEL THE LEAST CONFIDENT IN MY WORK IS WHEN I REMIND MYSELF TO JUST START. EVERY STITCH IS ANOTHER CHANCE TO PRACTICE AND LEARN. IT'S OKAY IF MY STITCHES AREN'T ALWAYS PERFECT; THE MAGIC CAN BE FOUND IN THE IMPERFECTIONS–AND IMPERFECTIONS ARE BEAUTIFUL."**
*–SARAH SCHILHABEL, LOVER OF NEEDLE CRAFTS AND IMPERFECTIONS*

So as you dig into what it means to see a whole creative project through from start to finish, whether it's small in scope or large, remember that there's no way it "should" feel, no amount of time it "should" take, no amount of confidence you "should" have.

All there is, really, is the showing up. The doing it. The playing and exploring. The trying new things. The making time to nurture your creative habit and keep commitments to yourself. The picking up tools, putting them down, trying different ones. From there, all you can do is wait to see what happens!

Though I have no idea what your process will look like in the actual making of a project, and there are lots of types of art I don't know much about, I *can* guess at some obstacles that might pop up, and I can share what I've learned about getting over, around, or through them. Read on.

# Failure: Nothing to Fear

Let's talk about the F word: *failure.*

*Failure* is a word people often use as a weapon against others, or we use it against ourselves. We might say or think, "I am a failure."

That's a very harsh thought about your identity, and also—it can't possibly be true. No one is "a failure." The things we do can fail, and sometimes we feel disappointed about our creative output, but *we* are *never* failures. We have inherent dignity and value. The more we can grasp that truth, the better it can carry us through the experience of failure.

Because yes, a creative project can be a failure. In fact, not only *can* a project fail; it *will* fail. And I'm here to tell you that it's nothing to be afraid of. Failure is and will always be a very faithful companion to the creative process, so you might as well accept it and make it your friend.

Rather than using the word *failure* as a weapon or accusation or identity, I think of it as a word to describe the distance

## "OF ALL THE LIARS IN THE WORLD, SOMETIMES THE WORST ARE OUR OWN FEARS."

### –RUDYARD KIPLING

between how we want our creative projects to turn out and how they actually turn out. Every project starts with an idea. And when it's an idea that lives inside your imagination, and you don't tell it to anyone or try to make it exist, it's perfect.

The only way to keep your idea in that perfect state—the *only* way to keep it completely safe from failure—is to leave it there.

The moment you start the work of bringing it out of your imagination and into some external expression, it fails. It just does!

When I wrote my first novel, I knew how it all worked in my head and what I wanted the end result to be. But I'd never written a book before, so I didn't know what I was doing! I had no clue how to fix the problems with my writing that sprung up like weeds all over the pages. When I compared the finished result to the idea in my mind, the *book* was a failure. It wasn't good enough to be published, and I didn't know how to make it better.

But *I* was not a failure. I'd set out to write a book, and I did! Then I succeeded in writing two more books that were also failures, before I wrote one that succeeded in getting published. That book wasn't perfect either. In some ways I was happy with how it turned out but in others I wasn't, and some people liked it and some didn't.

More than ten years and six additional books later, that's still how it goes.

**"ONE TRUTH I TRY TO BEAR IN MIND: IT WILL BE BAD UNTIL IT'S GOOD. MEANING: THE FIRST SCRIBBLES; THE FREE ASSOCIATING; THE FLAT, UNDERIMAGINED SCENES AND THE CLICHÉD DESCRIPTIONS OF ONE'S EARLY DRAFTS ARE NOT SIGNS OF FAILURE OR SIGNALS TO QUIT. THEY'RE AN ESSENTIAL PART OF THE PROCESS. THAT'S THE MESSY SCRATCHWORK YOU DO ON THE WAY TO A FINISHED PIECE. YOU CAN'T SPEW A POLISHED WORK OF FICTION FULL-BLOWN FROM YOUR FOREHEAD LIKE ZEUS."**

*—MARYROSE WOOD, AUTHOR OF ALICE'S FARM: A RABBIT'S TALE AND FOUNDER OF PATH OF THE STORYTELLER, OFFERING TOOLS AND TRAINING FOR WRITERS*

Every time I get a new idea for a book, it's perfect! It really is. It shines and shimmers in the light of my imagination. The story has no weak spots, and the characters are all complex but lovable. *This is the one, I think. This time, it will all pour out of me and stay perfect the whole way through.*

Spoiler alert: It is never the one. It never stays perfect.

Creating is a lot about translation. You're translating the thing in your imagination into your medium of choice: words, musical notes, paints, pixels, images, performance. That act of translation

**"GIVE YOURSELF PERMISSION TO WRITE SOMETHING TERRIBLE. IT DOESN'T MATTER IF IT'S GOOD. IT MATTERS IF IT'S ON THE PAGE. YOU CAN EDIT AND IMPROVE ANYTHING, BUT ONLY ONCE IT EXISTS!"**

**–MICOL OSTOW, AUTHOR**

is almost always imperfect. There's almost always distance between what's in your imagination and what comes out.

Every single one of my published books fails in some way to live up to what I wanted it to be. I do think that the more I write and the longer I practice, the better I get at closing the distance between my idea and the finished work. But then my ideas get more complicated too, and the gap widens once again.

I don't mean to minimize the fear of failure. It can be powerful! I've learned to live and work with failure sitting right next to me, but that doesn't mean I don't get afraid of it sometimes. That fear is at the root of a lot of the obstacles I and many others face when trying to show up for our creative practice, no matter how accomplished we might be or how many projects we've finished before. We may not even be conscious of it.

Here's how it can play out:

You write a sentence or line or paragraph or page, and almost immediately the mortification sets in. You look at it and think, *Oh no, oh no no no NO, this is not at all how that was supposed to come out.* You start your epic sketch of a flying horse and it's not going great, and a friend looks over your shoulder and you hunch down and cover your paper and hiss, "DON'T LOOK." You're working out a song on your guitar and your dad knocks on the door and says, "Hey, whatcha working on?" and you want to tell him to go away, *please, now.* Or you share your idea with a friend, who stares back at you with a skeptical look and says, "I don't get it."

It's often the idea of someone else seeing and judging what we're doing that aggravates the fear of failure, but it can also happen with just you alone in a room. Dealing with the reality of the distance between what you imagined and what it is can produce anxiety. It stirs up those feelings of failure—which we've been taught to be afraid of. We've been taught that failing is bad and something to be avoided, when in fact it is just part of the process.

**"SOMETIMES YOUR BEST CREATIVE MOVE IS DANGEROUSLY CLOSE TO YOUR WORST. YOU HAVE TO RISK POSSIBLE CREATIVE DISASTER TO DISCOVER TRUE CREATIVE ACHIEVEMENT. YOU MUST BE WILLING TO CREATIVELY FAIL IF YOU DARE REACH YOUR CREATIVE POTENTIAL."**

**–SCOTT DERRICKSON,
DIRECTOR OF MARVEL'S DOCTOR STRANGE**

**"SUCKING IS A VITAL PART OF THE PROCESS. THINK OF YOUR FAVORITE BOOK OR SONG OR PAINTING AND KNOW THAT AT SOME POINT IN THE LIFE OF THAT BOOK/SONG/PAINTING, IT SUCKED. THE ONLY REASON IT STOPPED SUCKING IS BECAUSE ITS CREATOR KEPT GOING UNTIL IT DIDN'T SUCK SO MUCH. ARTISTS AND WRITERS HAVE TO GIVE THEMSELVES PERMISSION TO SUCK."**

**–DAVID ARNOLD, AUTHOR**

Writers delete thousands of words of any given book while they write it. Songwriters throw out songs that aren't working. Directors do takes of a scene over and over, hoping to get closer to their vision every time. Dancers fall down, poets cut lines, actors don't get parts. We know from art historians that the artists we think of as the *best of all time* painted over their own paintings, each layer of paint a little history of failure. Think about the musician stumbling through a new piece, learning it, going over the hard parts again and again and again, memorizing it, all so they can bring it to life in a performance (and hope they don't forget any of it, which also happens sometimes).

You get the point.

Making something—getting a creative idea out of your head and into its skin, so to speak—is not easy. It's work. It can be fun work, it can be exciting work, and it can be scary and thrilling and messy and wonderful work, but it really is work.

And the point of this work isn't to avoid failure. (That's not the point of *life* either.)

The point is not control.

The point isn't to save yourself from embarrassment.

What *is* the point is something *I* cannot say, because it is very personal to *you*, something *you* get to decide for yourself. But whatever the point is for *you*, there's going to be lots of failure along the way. Failure is how we get wherever we're going. Failure is the road we walk on. We can't avoid it. It's inevitable. Without taking the risk of failure—practically running headlong into it!—there is no chance of getting that creative vision out of your imagination and into someone else's.

So you might as well make friends with failure! Get comfortable with it and try to accept the role it has in the creative process. And remember the most important thing: Experiencing creative failure does not mean you are "a failure."

# Resistance and Procrastination

Speaking of the fear of failure, it's a big part of what's going on when we procrastinate.

Procrastination is when you want to make the thing—you really, really do want to make the thing! You're excited about the thing, have planned for the thing, and have set aside some time to work on the thing. And then something happens in your brain, and you *don't do the thing*.

The thing suddenly feels impossible. You are convinced your idea is dumb and you're pretty sure you can't do it, and also you just happen to remember a dozen other things you should be doing instead, and organizing your closet sounds like a much better use of your time than working on your story or dance or song.

When it happens over and over, it might lead you to think: *Oh, maybe I'm not really a writer. Maybe I'm not actually creative. I guess if I wanted to it, I'd do it, but I'm not doing it, so I guess I'm a failu—wait, no I'm not. But I guess I'm just not meant to do this.*

Lies!

This phenomenon—of really, really wanting to do a thing but then repeatedly not doing it—is *very* common. In fact, if you follow any writers or other creative professionals on social media, or ever go to readings or festivals or events, or listen to podcast

interviews with artists, there's a good chance you've heard a writer say something like "I hate writing."

*What?!*

How is this possible? How does your favorite writer hate writing? Why do so many successful creative people have a problem with procrastination, and how did they manage to succeed while struggling with this?

As we've established, creative work is not easy.

You're making something from nothing! It's hard!

And humans have a natural resistance to doing things we perceive as hard because it causes discomfort and, basically, we are biologically wired to avoid discomfort.

Recently—*very* recently—okay, it was today—I was having a major struggle with getting to it when it was time for me to sit down and write. I work from home, and my work involves writing novels, writing books like this, writing short articles, writing content for companies, and sometimes teaching.

I was going to start work at ten a.m. after my usual morning routines: coffee, shower, breakfast, reading the news, going for a walk if it's nice out, that sort of thing. Then some work-related email came in, and though it wasn't urgent, I decided to just "get it out of the way." Then I chose to run to the store to get a couple of things that I'll need soon. (I don't need them *today*, but I know I'll need them *soon*, which is a very nonspecific time frame.)

When I got back from doing that, it was almost time to eat lunch. Not quite, but almost. Not enough time to start a whole *writing thing*. So I opted to do the dishes first, then I had lunch while I read a book, then I texted my friend about the book I was reading, then we started discussing the weather and bees and flies, which led to looking up some pictures and cartoons, then I took a quick look at the news again and then it was like 3:45.

*3:45!* How'd *that* happen?

I searched for some memes about the passage of time, distraction, procrastination, and writing. I was thinking I'd post something clever about how nearly six hours managed to slip away from me and shame myself into getting to work? I don't know.

I beat myself up a little.

Sara! Why are you like this? Why can't you just sit down and do the thing you know you want to do!

I texted a different friend. He asked me, had I tried making an outline?

I thought, *What a terrible and rude thing to say to someone who wants to commiserate about procrastinating!*

At about 4:30, I took my computer and lap desk and glass of water into my bedroom, put on some music, and told myself that it wasn't too late to keep my promise to myself and get my writing done. And I committed to myself that I would not check any news or internet things until six. Finally, I got writing.

Now, you probably won't have exactly this problem. Probably a lot of your day is taken up by school or work or maybe both. You might also have homework and/or chores, and maybe sports or other extracurriculars, meaning there is less time to waste.

(By the way, having less time to waste can be a good thing. It can really light a fire under you because you know your time is limited, and you know that when it comes time for your creativity appointment, it's now or never. A lot of writers I know who are also parents of small kids or who have other jobs manage to get quite a bit done in whatever small window of time they have in a day, because the limits help them focus.)

For better or for worse, I have lots of free time, and today was a particularly acute example of what happens to me when I'm really resisting getting to my writing. Not every day is like this, but I've had enough of these days over my last twelve years of being an author to know that resistance is not something I can just conquer with better habits or more willpower. It takes a lot of different strategies for me to circumvent or fool that part of me that is like a stubborn toddler saying *no no no no no no no no no no no* for reasons I am only semi-conscious of.

So, if you keep not doing the creative thing you know you want to do, the good news is that this is a totally common part of the creative process. The bad news is . . . wait, there's no bad news here! Maybe just *uncomfortable* news. Which is that though resistance and procrastination are normal for most artists, we still have to find ways around it and through it so we can get the thing done. And there is no one-size-fits-all way to deal with it.

In the next chapters, I'll share some of the various things others and I use when we find ourselves having One of Those Days.

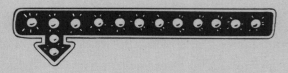

*"Writer's Block"?*

*When I'm out visiting schools and talking to groups, it seems like at every event someone raises their hand and asks me if I get "writer's block." For some reason, the concept of writer's block is familiar to audiences of all ages. Personally, I never use the phrase "writer's block" to describe the challenges I have with writing. It's my opinion that what a lot of people call writer's block is usually some mix of fear, perfectionism, and resistance. It might also be that you aren't ready to jump into the project itself yet, and you need to do a little more brainstorming or outlining. For me, it's not helpful to give my challenges a name like "writer's block" because that sounds like some condition that I can't do anything about,* and also, it's not very specific. It's better for me to say, "I feel like I don't know what I'm doing," or "I don't know what should happen next in my story," or "I feel lazy today and would rather watch some shows," or "This feels like homework," or whatever else the issue is.

I asked my friend Jennifer Lynn Barnes about this. She's not only a writer (of Inheritance Game and The Naturals); she's also a PhD with degrees in psychology, psychiatry, and cognitive science. She knows a lot about human behavior! She says:

"For me, there are three kinds of creative block. The first kind happens because I'm run down. My tank is empty, and I need to refill. The second kind happens because I have taken a wrong step somewhere along the way, and I can't move forward until I backtrack and figure out what isn't working. And the third kind of block is really just my brain's way of saying, 'This is hard,' and then I just have to remind myself that creating is indeed hard, that it is sometimes supposed to be hard. The key for me is figuring out what kind of block I am facing, because forcing myself to keep working and push through won't do a thing for me in the first two cases, and it is the only solution to the last."

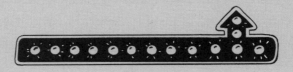

# Warmups!

## WORD WARMUPS

If you've ever played or watched sports, you know that runners don't just run out onto the field and take off in a hundred-yard dash. Pitchers don't walk out to the mound and throw their first pitch of the day in the actual game. Quarterbacks run drills with their receivers, and soccer players dribble and pass before a game and on the sideline when they're not on the field.

Athletes warm up.

Likewise, musicians tune their instruments and play some scales and short exercises before they start playing the piece of music they're there to perform. Actors and singers do vocal exercises and jump around and make funny noises so they don't strain their vocal cords when it's time to perform.

Writers also need to warm up!

Author Bret Anthony Johnston says that warmups "heighten concentration [and] awaken creativity. . . . They make it easier to get your butt in the chair, and to keep it there."[4]

Writing warmups are related to freewrites, but a little different. Where freewriting is a bit of mental leaf-raking for any kind of creative practice, or just for use in *life*, writing warmups are specifically for the *practice* of writing and getting the

---

4 Bret Anthony Johnston, Naming the World, p. 332.

language center of your brain engaged and ready to access the thousands of words that are there waiting to be put to good use. Here's how writing warmups work:

1. Get out a piece of paper or a notebook and something to write with. (You *can* do this on a computer, but if you are able to write by hand, I recommend it.)

2. Find something you can time yourself with: kitchen timer, phone, watch, etc.

3. Pick one of the warmups below, and set your timer for two minutes. Go! Don't stop to think. Try to keep your pen, pencil, or fingers moving the whole time.

- Write down every word you can think of that starts with the letter *T*.

- Write down everything you can think of that is in your kitchen.

- Write down the name of every fruit and vegetable you can think of.

- For two minutes, write a description of your favorite teacher.

- Describe your own bedroom. Use the whole two minutes! Think of every detail you can.

- Write about a recent dream you had, and see how much you can remember.

- Write all the words you can think of that have to do with trees. (*Leaves, bark, Christmas,* and . . . ?)

- Write a list of things you can find in the freezer section of a grocery store.

You get the idea. You can cycle through these as many times as you want, replacing the letters of the alphabet, the rooms in your house, the sections of the supermarket, etc.

## DRAWING WARMUPS

My artist friends tell me that painters and other visual artists use their own versions of warmups. Here are some examples:

- Sketch a page of basic shapes—circles, squares, triangles—to get your brain to start thinking visually and get your mind/body connection crackling.

- Play with color using your paints or crayons.

- Sketch what you see in front of you right now.

- Pick an "animal of the day" and draw it as fast as you can. Remember, this is about loosening up, not about making it good!

If you run out of warmups for the kind of art that you do, there are tons of resources out there, from books to websites to email newsletters. Try search terms like "writing prompts," "art warmups," and "creativity warmups." You'll also find a list of resources at the end of this book. You can build a whole little library or folder full of ideas for prompts and warmups.

What do warmups have to do with procrastination, resistance, and fear?

A lot of our resistance has to do with the discomfort of transitioning from one task or state to another. From not writing to writing. From watching a video to making one. From anxious staring to purposeful work. Warmups help ease that transition. A list of words or describing a room? Not too scary! Drawing a bunch of circles? Can do! You might really be amazed at how these simple tasks can build a bridge for you to get from not doing to doing. The following exercises are other ways to do that.

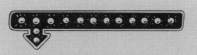

*Fun fact! Depending on how old you are, you've got anywhere from about 5,000 to 30,000 words all up in your brain. Writing warmups can help shake them out!*

## TWELVE MINUTES

Some days this will happen: I show up, I'm ready, I'm warmed up, and . . . I still don't *do the thing*. When this happens, I put that timer to use again. I tell myself I only have to do the thing for twelve minutes. Twelve solid, focused minutes. Then, if I still can't get into it, I can stop trying.

You might prefer eight minutes or fifteen minutes. The exact amount of time doesn't matter that much. The point is to decide on and commit to a length of time that is not so short that it feels pointless or so long that it feels scary.

Get your workspace set up, turn off your notifications, put on music if you like, and set a timer. Then get writing or drawing or storyboarding or dancing or whatever your thing is.

Usually, by the time my twelve minutes are up, I am unstuck. The resistance and dread have been completely deflated, and I can keep going for an hour or so and meet whatever my goal is for that day.

And if that doesn't happen? I still reap the benefits of making a commitment—even just a twelve-minute commitment—and sticking to it. It's a boost to my self-esteem and a signal to myself that being creative is an important part of who I am, and that even on days when it feels almost impossible, I can still give myself twelve minutes. Which is twelve minutes more than I would have done if I hadn't tried!

# Change of Scenery

If I've been sitting at the kitchen table for the whole day checking news, searching for memes, and writing to-do lists, that's probably not going to magically be the perfect spot now for working on my novel. And if I've been sitting at my desk dealing with bills and emails or doing work for a business client, that may not be where my creative energy gets flowing.

I know this seems very basic, but simply getting up and moving to a different location in the house or even a different spot in the same room can have a surprisingly powerful effect on being able to transition to your project.

Today I spent a lot of my goofing-around time at the kitchen table. The kitchen table is also where I like to write sometimes, but once that location became my goofing-off spot for the day, it was no longer useful as a writing spot. The dining-room table is another good writing place, but yesterday I spent hours doing some boring business writing for a client at that table. I also like the living room, but last night I watched way too much TV in there, and it would be so easy to turn it back on.

That only left the bedroom and the bathroom. (I went with the bedroom, but I do have friends who have turned the bathroom into a writing spot when it's the only place no one will bother them!) I hardly ever write in the bedroom, but relocating to the bed was a drastic enough change to get my brain to shift gears from "I was not writing" to "*Now* I *am* writing."

This is just an example of a change of scenery inside the house. If it's an option for you, going to a park or a coffee shop or a library to work on your project can also provide a great change of scenery.

# Movement Break

A movement break does a similar thing as a change of scenery, except that with a movement break, you're going to totally stop the attempt at creativity. You're not doing it to get involved in another task or get caught up on your devices, but to engage your body in movement, as you are able.

I like to dance when I'm alone (in front of people is another story!), so sometimes for me, a movement break is putting on a great song or two and dancing around my living room without worrying what I look like doing it. I fully get into it.

Another thing I like is going for short walks. I like long walks too, but not for a movement break. I don't want to take too much time for this kind of break. I'll just grab my keys and walk around the block or the neighborhood for fifteen minutes at the most.

Stretching is also good. Stretching, dancing, walking, breathing, rolling your neck around, flexing your ankles— whatever you like and are able to do.

What is the point of this? It shakes you up. Sometimes the frustration of trying to wrestle a creative vision out of your head and onto the paper or canvas is like being stuck in a loop. You try, and you can't; you try, and you can't; you try, and you can't. Or you keep almost starting, then not; almost starting, then not. Movement disrupts the loop. Like all of these exercises, it can help unstick you. The bonus benefit of movement is that it gets your blood flowing and transporting oxygen and nutrients to your brain. Writing, editing, playing an instrument, using your voice, painting, drawing—these are all physical things too, yet we can get trapped in our thoughts while doing them.

A movement break re-engages that mind-body connection.

"AS AN AUTISTIC PERSON, I TEND TO GET STUCK IN MY HEAD, SO IN ORDER TO CREATE, I NEED TO GET OUT OF MY HEAD AND INTO THE WORLD. ONE SIMPLE THING I DO IS TAKE A THANKFULNESS WALK. YOU JUST WALK A FEW BLOCKS IN YOUR NEIGHBORHOOD, GIVING THANKS FOR TREES, FOR A PORCH THAT LOOKS INVITING, FOR THE SMELL OF COOKING COMING FROM THE MEXICAN RESTAURANT, FOR KIDS RIDING BIKES, FOR THE SLUMPING RUINS OF AN OLD RED BARN ON THE EDGE OF TOWN. JUST TUNE IN AND FIND AS MANY SPECIFIC DETAILS AS YOU CAN, AND FOR EACH ONE, SAY, 'THANK YOU' TO GOD OR THE UNIVERSE OR THE HUMAN FAMILY OR WHATEVER YOU LIKE.

WHEN I GET HOME, I'M FEELING, INSTEAD OF JUST THINKING ABOUT THINGS. THIS IS BECAUSE SENSORY INPUT IS PROCESSED IN THE LIMBIC SYSTEM OF THE BRAIN. THESE DETAILS DON'T HIT YOU ONLY IN THE MIND; THEY GET TO YOUR HEART AND GUT. AS I'M FEELING MY FEELINGS, THE DETAILS I OBSERVED OFTEN SUGGEST A PAST, A STORY. IF YOU'RE AN ARTIST, YOU'LL PROBABLY FIND YOURSELF THINKING ABOUT THOSE STORIES, AND WANTING TO WRITE A POEM OR SONG OR JOURNAL ENTRY, OR PAINT OR DRAW AN IMAGE THAT STANDS OUT FOR YOU. ALSO, YOU MIGHT FIND THAT YOU'RE SIMPLY IN A BETTER, MORE CHARITABLE MOOD TOWARD THE WORLD AND EVEN TOWARD YOURSELF."

**—DANIEL BOWMAN JR., WRITER**

# Make Something Else

If you're working on an epic project that you've been thinking about for a long time and that means a lot to you, you've probably built up a lot of expectations in your mind about what doing it will feel like and how it will turn out. High expectations aren't a bad thing; neither is ambition.

That said, if you are a person prone to anxiety, sometimes those expectations end up creating pressure. We know we're capable of working under a certain amount of pressure. We do it at finals time and on test days, on game days and performance days, and anytime there's an external or internal expectation going on.

But sometimes the pressure gets too intense, to the point where it's no longer a positive force giving us just the right amount of push but instead becomes a bit of a bully. When it feels like that, *not* doing your creative thing is always an option. You might really need a day off. Sometimes though, that can feel defeating. I might not feel up to the project that's all wrapped up with my every hope and dream, but I still want to tap into my creative writer–self and *make* something. I don't want to be bullied into completely backing down.

That's when I just make something else.

I take my creative time and energy back from the pressure and expectations and give it something manageable to focus on—something I don't care about *quite* so much. I might take a back-burner project and give it the front burner for the day, or pull out notes I have on a "might be interesting someday" project and add to them.

Instead of chapter three of your epic fantasy series, write a little bit of that idea for a short story you've been thinking about, or use a writing prompt to get a few paragraphs of *anything* out.

Instead of working on the three-act musical about Spiderman, try writing a simple eight-line poem about your cat.

Instead of working on your album of all original songs, have fun recording some covers.

Play with something creative that is not so burdened with your ideas and expectations about what it *should* be and how it will be the best thing ever written by you or anyone else.

Pretty soon, the chatter shuts up and the pressure has been released. Chances are, you'll get far enough into it to unfreeze and slide into the epic thing you wanted to work on in the first place. And if not, you still will have produced something new. Awesome!

 **"MY MANTRA IS: WORK FAST, WORK MESSY, LEAVE YOUR EDITING VOICE BEHIND. ALLOW YOUR WRITING TO SUCK. TAKE LEAPS OF FAITH, EVEN IF YOU KNOW IT DOESN'T WORK! IT'S ALL ABOUT MOMENTUM—KEEP MOVING FORWARD, YOU'LL FIX IT LATER. HAVE FUN WITH IT. FORGET ALL YOUR RESEARCH AND PLOT POINTS. THE MEMORABLE STUFF WILL RISE TO THE SURFACE. TRUST YOURSELF, TRUST YOUR GUT—DON'T STOP TO THINK TOO HARD! DON'T LOOK BACK TILL YOU GET TO THE END. THEN PUT IT AWAY AND GO SEE A MOVIE OR TWO. LIE IN THE GRASS, HUG A TREE, EMPTY YOUR HEAD. WHEN YOU'RE READY, TAKE A LOOK: YOU JUST MIGHT BE SURPRISED HOW MUCH OF IT IS GOOD!"**
**–G. NERI, AUTHOR**

# Dessert First

Often when we are creating anything narrative—meaning something that tells a story with a beginning, middle, and end, like a novel or play or movie or musical—we tend to write it in linear sequence. That is, we start at the beginning and create it in order until we get to the end. That makes sense and is a good way to tell a story, but it's not the only way.

If you're stuck and procrastinating and resistant, the problem might just be that you don't know what happens next in your story. Or you know what happens next, but you also know it's complicated and you don't really know yet how to make it work. Or you know what happens next, but it's a little boring and you'd really rather write the action scene that comes in chapter ten because you know it's going to be fun and exciting and you've been imagining it for weeks.

Go ahead! Do the fun part!

No one is watching, and you aren't going to get in trouble for not doing it in order.

Skip ahead to the part you really enjoy.

Sing the part of the song that is your favorite.

Write the car chase.

Play the big guitar solo.

This will remind you that exercising your creativity isn't some should-do chore like algebra homework or mowing the lawn. You are *making* something that only you can make, and it's *for you*—a chance to connect with yourself, express yourself, understand yourself. Then after you loosen up and do the fun part, you will probably find yourself a lot less scared about the parts that may be a little more daunting but that are necessary to put your whole project together.

# Self-Doubt— a.k.a. "What Am I Even Doing?"

So you've been working on your project for a while and you've learned how to get around some procrastination and resistance, but you still have these days when:

- the paints and brushes sit there.

- the blank page stares back from your notebook or screen.

- the guitar watches you from where it leans in the corner, judging.

- the story you imagine in your head won't come out.

- And all you can think is, *What am I even doing?*

It feels different than procrastination. It's not even fear of failure. It's something deeper, more about identity and purpose. It feels like this thing that's supposed to be fun, that's supposed to give you joy, that's supposed to be your personal space to be *you* and get all the awesome stuff in your brain into some creative form is just . . . impossible and embarrassing and *soooo* awkward and maybe even painful and, like, why did you even ever think you could try?

This is self-doubt.

Self-doubt is that scary sense that you don't even like to acknowledge is there, a lack of confidence that goes bone-deep. It's about more than creativity. It's about you and your worth. It can express itself strongly in the midst of creative practice by saying: "You're a fake and a fraud and *you can't do this.*"

It can be a big, scary feeling, and I'm not going to tell you how to make it go away forever because *I* don't know how. I still get that feeling sometimes—more than I want to or expected to this far into my life as a writer and a human being.

What I can tell you about that feeling from over twenty years of writing and nearly fifty years of life is this:

- It's normal and common.

- It *doesn't* mean you shouldn't do your practice or carry on with whatever you're doing.

- You *can* survive feeling this way.

The thing about creating is that it's pretty much all new, every time. That is the very nature of the act of creating—indeed, of the word *create*. You're making something that wasn't there before. Bringing into existence a thing—a line, a melody, a dance, a drawing, an interpretation—that did not exist until you did it.

And actually, that's kind of true about life.

Have you ever lived your life before? Has anyone else?

Living life is a continual act of creation. Everything is new, all the time. We don't always see it because we get into patterns and habits, and there are things and people around us that become familiar. Our problems can feel repetitive, our challenges the same as they were yesterday. Yet every minute is a new one that hasn't been lived before exactly the way we're going to live it.

And that can sometimes feel difficult and frightening. We don't feel up to it. Our self-doubt gets stirred up: *What if I make a mistake? What if I am a mistake? What if I don't belong here?*

Sometimes getting into our creative selves brings these fears and questions to light in a new way, and that's what can make it so hard sometimes to just get some sentences down or to sit down and do anything.

You will *make* mistakes; making mistakes is human.

But *you* are *not* a mistake.

You *do* belong here.

And you're not alone.

In fact, you're in great company when it comes to feeling confused, inadequate, or scared. It's not about being young and inexperienced, if that's what you are. People who create for a living and have been doing it for years—decades, even!—also struggle with deep self-doubts and the regular questioning of our identity as artists and people.

I do. Most artists I know do too, at least some of the time. And we've learned that the feeling of self-doubt is *not* a sign that you can't or shouldn't do it. It's not a sign you're "not gifted" or "not talented" or "not creative" or "not inspired" or any other "nots" that we throw around to identify and label others or ourselves.

We can survive the self-doubts and all the feelings that come with them, whether they crop up in the practice of creativity or in the process of simply living.

**"YOU KNOW THAT VOICE INSIDE YOUR HEAD THAT STARTS TALKING WHEN YOU'RE MAYBE HALFWAY DONE WITH YOUR PROJECT? THE ONE THAT TELLS YOU THAT EVERYTHING YOU'VE DONE IS TRASH, THAT YOU SHOULD GO WORK ON SOMETHING ELSE, THAT YOU'RE NO GOOD? I'VE LEARNED THAT (1) THE VOICE NEVER GOES AWAY NO MATTER HOW OLD YOU GET, AND (2) THE VOICE IS ALWAYS LYING. ALWAYS."**

*—GENE LUEN YANG, WRITER AND CREATOR OF GRAPHIC NOVELS AND COMIC BOOKS*

# The Trouble with Expectations—Yours

Underlying self-doubt (and a lot of the challenges we have in our creative practice) is a thing called *expectations*. An expectation is an assumption, a belief. In this case, it's about what you expect to happen or how you expect to feel or ways you expect other people to react to you and your work.

If you *expect* creativity to always flow or to come from inspiration, and it doesn't, your self-doubt can get triggered. If you *expect* that doing one good painting means you'll always do good paintings, and then it doesn't work out that way, you might question your identity.

When I officially became a published, full-time writer, I had a lot of expectations around how that would feel. I expected to feel confident. I expected to wake up in the mornings full of joy and excitement because I was living the dream doing the only job I ever wanted that much.

And then, when I didn't feel confidence, joy, and excitement nearly as often as I thought I would, I was a lot more vulnerable to sliding into a pit of fear and self-doubt. I worried that maybe I wasn't meant for the writing life. Maybe I wasn't any good. Did I even know how stories worked? In the beginning of my professional writing career, I did a lot of crying.

I can still see myself lying on my kitchen floor, staring at the ceiling with tears slipping down my cheeks, thinking, *I am going to fail. I'm not a real writer. I'm going to let everyone down. I don't know how to write a book. I will be criticized, and I can't handle it.*

When I wasn't crying on the kitchen floor, I was crying on the couch. I was crying in bed. I was crying at my desk. It . . . was a lot of crying! Which was very different from my expectation that I would sit in coffee shops or at my kitchen table or at my desk, typing away on my laptop or writing by hand in a notebook—inspired yet peaceful, focused and serene, energetic and capable and basically bubbling over with the ABSOLUTE JOY OF DOING WHAT I LOVE!

It threw me off for a while. But as I've talked to other writers and creative people and learned that *all* of them, at least sometimes, hate doing what they love, I've started to accept that my expectations were not based in reality. The difficulties of creating are part of the deal, part of the process, and I try not to give them too much power to throw me off track.

Do you have expectations about what you think creating is "supposed to" feel like? What it's supposed to look like? *Be like?* I think we all do. And in some ways, being able to accept the difference between those expectations and reality is the most important skill in sustaining a creative practice for life.

The reality is that no matter how good you get, no matter how much experience you gain, and no matter how many signs of success you experience, there will be . . .

- crying days and days when you feel elated and days that are just blah.

- days when creating actually feels *bad* and you wonder why you're doing it, right next to days when you know *exactly* why you're doing it and it feels fine or great!

- days when you can't stop thinking that you'll never finish what you're making, and days when you have total confidence that you will

It's natural to have expectations. Everybody does. But when they smack into reality with a loud and painful crash, it can throw us off. It's all part of the process, and you're not alone.

# The Trouble with Expectations—Other People's

On top of the internal expectations we might have about a creative practice, there's another type of expectations that can affect us. Those are the expectations of the People Out There. For me, the People Out There are people who read my books, my agent, my editor, my friends, my mother, reviewers, Amazon shoppers, Goodreads users, other writers.

When I first started writing, there were no People Out There. I was the only one who knew I was writing or cared if I did it or not. Then I joined a writers group, and the number of People Out There increased, but only slightly. All that my writers group (about seven people) cared about was whether I submitted writing for us to discuss when I was supposed to. They were there to give helpful feedback while eating snacks, and their expectations were very manageable.

Outside of that, no one knew I existed as a writer. Very few people cared whether I wrote a book! *I* was the only person who cared.

For me, that changed after publication, and it can change anytime you put something out into the world for other people to read or watch or listen to.

Suddenly, there were a whole bunch of People Out There who had either an emotional or a financial investment in what I wrote next. People ranking my book on a scale of one to five. People to please or disappoint. People tracking how many copies I sold. People telling me when I needed to finish and turn in my next draft.

It was a *lot*!

The People Out There and their expectations were in my thoughts all the time, and it took genuine effort to shut them up and kick them out when it was time to create. *Takes*, I should say, not *took*, because though I've learned that I can't let them into my creative process, the People Out There and their expectations still exist. I'm better and better at closing the curtain for privacy during my personal creative time so I can focus on my own gut and creative goals.

That said, is there a time and a place for pulling back the curtain? I say yes.

Let's talk about sharing your work.

We live in a world where sharing has become a pretty huge part of life. Almost every action we take or thought we have is easily shareable with any number of sites or apps, and is then subject to views and likes and reactions and re-sharing. In fact, it's kind of unusual and countercultural these days to *not* share, though there's definitely value, too, in being private.

It is, however, a natural human impulse to share.

*See me! Know me! Understand me! I exist too!*

That's part of why we create—to make a declaration of who we are, what we think, what we care about, what we can do, what we have to offer and express. People have been leaving their creative mark for millennia, from cave paintings and artifacts and writing

**"THERE'S SOMETHING MAGICAL THAT HAPPENS WHEN I SHARE MY WORK WITH OTHERS. AS SOON AS I HAND THEM THE SCRIPT, OR HIT 'SEND' ON THAT EMAIL . . . I SEE MY STORY FROM AN ENTIRELY NEW PERSPECTIVE. SOMETHING IN THE LITERAL ACT OF GIVING MY WORK AWAY CAUSES A SHIFT IN MY BRAIN. OFTEN, THE SIMPLE ACT OF SHARING THE WORK IS AS INSTRUCTIVE FOR ME AS ANY NOTES THAT COME FROM THE READERS. IT'S AN IMPERATIVE PART OF THE PROCESS."**

**–SCOTT TEEMS, WRITER-DIRECTOR**

on stone tablets to photographs and letters and memoirs viewed on digital tablets.

Sharing is also an important part of growing as an artist, if that's one of your goals. Constructive criticism from people who are farther along the path than we are is very valuable. Seeing our work through someone else's eyes is a good way to understand our strengths and challenges. Taking workshops and classes, doing lessons, engaging in one-on-one mentorship, and getting peer feedback are all ways we learn.

Sharing isn't easy, of course. It opens us up to judgment and can trigger our fears of inadequacy, or of being misunderstood. In the right setting and at the right time, I think the risks of sharing are worth the potential benefits. In this section, I'll go over what I've learned about when, how, and with whom to share your creative output, and what to do with the responses.

# When?

How do you know when it's time to share your work? It's not always easy to tell. The more you do it, the better you get at knowing on a gut level that you're ready to open the curtains on a particular project. But when you're starting out, you tend to learn this by trial and error. There have been times I shared too soon, when my idea was too fragile and I was vulnerable to getting scared off of it if the feedback wasn't enthusiastically positive. And there have been times I shared too late, when my deadline was getting close and I didn't really have time to incorporate helpful suggestions.

Here are some signs that you might be ready to share something you made or are in the process of making:

- You feel you need encouragement.

- You're stuck or frustrated, and you need ideas for how to proceed or solve a problem.

- You can tell you've gotten as far as you can on your own. It's good, but you know it can be better, and you'd like some expert advice.

- You decide you'd like a collaborator or collaborators for the project and want to invite more people into it.

- You've finished. You're done with the project and are ready to put it out into the world and let it go!

# How and with Whom?

You can share your work in a lot of different ways, and which ones you choose will have a lot to do with why and when you're sharing. As easy as it is to post your work online with a single click or tap, I recommend giving some thought to how you're sharing and who is going to see it rather than to share it on impulse with the entire world. The more you've invested in the project, the more thought is required.

Here are some reasons some people choose to share their work; maybe one or more will resonate with you:

**For practice and accountability:** I follow some visual artists and craftspeople on Instagram, and many have a "do art every day" kind of approach, where they have decided to sketch or stitch or paint or write every day and post their creation publicly right away. Their goals are often about giving themselves a low- or no-pressure creative assignment, doing it, and being done with it. The sharing is to say "I did it" and move on to the next thing. I think social media is perfect for this. They aren't looking for feedback, and they aren't deeply emotionally invested in the work. It's about the practice and maybe the accountability of having done it. The end.

**For help, encouragement, or constructive criticism:** For sharing with these types of objectives, a more "closed" version makes sense. That could be sharing with a writers group, an artists circle, a bandmate, or a set of trusted friends. There are a couple of things to consider before you do this type of sharing:

*Trust* is important. To share creative work is to be vulnerable, and not everyone has earned your vulnerability. The more of yourself you've put into your project, the more time you've invested, and the more obstacles you've had to overcome, the more vulnerable sharing will probably feel.

*Communication* is also very important! You can avoid a lot of issues by clearly communicating what you expect from the people you are sharing your work with. I remember the first time I sent some writing to another writer. I had no experience with feedback or writers groups or anything. I don't know what I expected, but when I got it back with his changes and comments all over it, I was so angry that I cried. I felt violated! I had just wanted him to read it and give me some general comments, not *write* all over my pages! After that, I learned to say what I was looking for whenever I shared my work with mentors or peers or loved ones.

For example:

**"I'm just looking for some nonspecific encouragement."**
This is what I call the "Good job, honey!" kind of feedback. This is a good thing to get from people you know love you. They don't have to know anything about the kind of art you're doing because all they need to say is some variation of "Wow, this is so neat! I'm proud of you! Keep going!"

**"This is my first draft, and I wonder if you would read it and give me your general first impressions about the overall story."** This is the type of thing you could ask of a writers group or a friend who is also a writer. If you're a painter, you would ask other painters. If a musician, other musicians. Et cetera. You don't need to be close friends with them; you just need to trust them and respect their opinions.

**"I know the story has some good points and some weak spots. Right now I just want to know if the ending works."** See how specific that is? Depending on what kind of art you do, the details will vary, but you get the idea. Being specific with your request means you're more likely to get the kind of targeted advice you're looking for.

**"This is my fifth draft of this, and I think I'd like to try to get it published/produced/recorded. Would you take a look at it and tell me what you think?"** This is also specific but is a more open invitation to serious critique, the kind of thing you would ask of a mentor or someone farther along in reaching the goals you have for your own work.

Two things to remember when you're looking for help, advice, and encouragement:

1. People might say no or might not quite give you what you asked for. That's one of the risks involved in sharing. The person or people you ask might be busy or might have

other reasons to say no. Also, no matter how specific you are or how you've gauged your trust level, sometimes people will overstep. When that happens, you get to decide if you'd like to try sharing with them again or not.

2. It's good manners to say thank you and to be willing to reciprocate. When you ask for feedback, you can offer to swap work or to provide feedback for them sometime in the future. And even if you don't like what you heard in feedback, or if you thought that it was way off base or that your work was totally misunderstood, say thank you anyway because someone gave their time to try to help.

**"THE BEST THING ABOUT FAILURE IS HOW FEW PEOPLE ACTUALLY SEE IT. I THINK WE'RE AFRAID OF FAILING BECAUSE WE THINK THE WHOLE WORLD IS GOING TO POINT AND LAUGH. BUT IN REALITY, OFTEN ONLY YOU KNOW THAT YOUR DREAM WOUND UP IN A DITCH. THAT MEANS YOU CAN KEEP IT TO YOURSELF, OR SHARE IT WITH PEOPLE YOU TRUST WITH YOUR VULNERABLE FEELINGS. AND THEN YOU CAN MOVE ON, AND THE WHOLE WIDE WORLD WILL SEE YOU AS SOMEONE WHO JUST KEEPS MOVING, WORKING, AND TRYING NEW THINGS."**

**—SARAH ENNI, WRITER AND PODCASTER**

# Then What?

Once you've tried sharing and asking for feedback, what do you do with all the input you've received? What if you don't like it? What if it didn't help? What if you feel worse? If the feedback isn't all positive, does that mean you and your work are worthless? How do you pick yourself back up to make something again?

Let me tell you something about me: I am the queen of avoiding criticism. I am so afraid of it. I'm a perfectionist and I struggle with self-doubt, and sometimes I feel like anything less than gushing enthusiasm from the entire world will absolutely crush me. Personally, I never ever look at things like Amazon or Goodreads reviews. A lot of my author friends do, but I can't handle it, and I figure there's no reason to look when it's too late for me to do anything about the thing being reviewed anyway. But with the things I know I do need to look at, like notes from my editor or student evaluations from a class I taught, or when I need to look at book sales reports . . . it all makes me want to run and hide.

And yet here I am, uncrushed and still writing. As with feelings of failure and self-doubt, I can survive the extreme but temporary discomfort and fear of criticism and bounce back from it, even if in the moment I think I won't.

The key to this is to remember that you get to decide what criticism to take in and what to let go of. As you get feedback, you start to learn to sort through it and categorize it in various piles, such as:

- Definitely helpful
- Something to consider
- Interesting but not what I'm looking for or doesn't feel right
- Not helpful
- Just plain mean!

You hold on to what is helpful or worth considering, and you learn to let go of the rest. And if you learn that it's way too hard for you to let go of the unhelpful and mean feedback, you might take a break from sharing until you build up your own sense of confidence again, or confine sharing to one very trusted person.

Sometimes you hear creative professionals talk about the need for a "thick skin." As someone who still hasn't developed a thick skin after twenty years of getting feedback, I don't think it's a requirement. It's okay to be sensitive. I know I am. And that might mean it takes some of us a little longer to bounce back, or we have to give ourselves a couple of days off to cry or feel hurt, or we become very selective about who we share with, or all of the above. There's nothing wrong with any of that, and it doesn't disqualify you from having a creative practice, sharing your work, or even becoming someone who does it for a living someday.

**"YOU CANNOT CONTROL THE WAY THE WORLD RECEIVES YOUR ART, WHETHER IT LANDS WITH A SMASH OR A BANG OR A BLIP OR EVEN A WHIFF. ALL YOU CAN DO IS CONTINUE TO WORK HARD AT MAKING NEW THINGS, KNOWING THAT THE MORE YOU MAKE, THE BETTER YOU WILL UNDERSTAND YOUR PROCESS AND YOUR STRENGTHS AS AN ARTIST, WHICH WILL THEN, IN ALL LIKELIHOOD, LEAD YOU TO MAKE EVEN BETTER THINGS."**
*–LANCE RUBIN, AUTHOR/WRITER/ACTOR/MUSICIAN*

The creative cycle isn't linear. It doesn't continue in a straight line forever, and it's not steps one, two, three, four in any kind of predictable order. As I said earlier, creativity is a cycle that tends to be more circular, or sometimes like a maze. More often than not, we find ourselves returning to the beginning over and over, to start again. And it comes back to play. Here are some of my final thoughts and suggestions about how we continue to start over and make things new again.

# Rest and Boredom

Do you know the story of how Lin-Manuel Miranda came up with the idea for the Broadway musical *Hamilton*?

He was on vacation, taking a break from performing in his first musical, *In the Heights*. And you can imagine he needed a break—performing on Broadway is exhausting! Casts do up to eight performances a week for months at a time, sometimes years, and they try to make the show great for every single audience. I can only imagine how burned out the performers in hit shows must get.

Anyway, there he was, looking for a way to relax. He bought a big book to escape into on vacation and climbed into his hammock with it. That book was the biography *Alexander Hamilton* by Ron Chernow. Not even fifty pages into it, Miranda started imagining Hamilton's life as a play or a musical. And then he went on to create one of the biggest Broadway sensations in modern history.

I love that story! It's a powerful lesson about what can come when we actually let ourselves rest.

Sometimes creativity is about good habits and routines and not waiting around to be inspired. It can be about discipline and putting in the time and effort to get the results we want.

But even the most prolific, award-winning, and popular singers, actors, and writers can't be all hustle all the time. A lot of people, including me, believe that your creativity can get dried up. Your tank can wind up on empty. You can practice great habits and discipline and try to come up with ideas and put down words, and then one day find there's nothing there to give.

So what do you do when your creative tank is empty? How do you fill it back up so there's something in there to draw from?

Maybe you can't take a beach vacation like Lin-Manuel Miranda or, for that matter, any kind of trip in the traditional sense—getting on a plane and staying in a hotel, leaving your homework or your job or your regular life behind.

But you *can* rest.

Everyone has different needs and ideas about what is restful. It depends on personality, lifestyle, preferences, and what your real-world options actually are. What comes to your mind when you think of rest, relaxation, unwinding, taking a break, recharging? What does it look like for you?

For me, there is fake rest and there is real rest.

Fake rest is when I say, "I'm going to take a few days off from writing," and then I spend that time on social media while simultaneously binge-watching shows I don't even like that much. Or I fill the time up with checking things off a demanding to-do list. Or I stare at my phone all day, scrolling through Instagram and feeling inadequate, or scrolling through the news and feeling anxious.

Sure, I may be taking a break from writing, but am I really *resting*? Am I going to feel refreshed and ready to engage with creativity again after days like that? Probably not. Do I make this mistake over and over again anyway? Yes!

Another kind of fake rest I'm really good at is pretending to myself that I am going to write "soon," even though I kind of have a gut feeling I'm not going to, no matter what I try to do in order to break through my resistance.

Any second now, I tell myself, *I will sit down and get into my writing.*

*In five minutes.*

*After coffee.*

*At eleven.*

*After lunch.*

*Before dinner.*

*After my walk.*

*After I do the dishes.*

*Before bed.*

I do all my little tricks to try to get myself to write, but it isn't going to happen, and I know it. Meanwhile, throughout the day I'm beating myself up that I'm not writing. I can go down a very slippery slope of telling myself I'm a lazy loser, asking myself why I can't get myself together and just do it, wondering how I ever thought I could write in the first place, lamenting that I don't deserve my career, etc., etc., etc.

Then there I am at the end of the day, sitting in a cloudy, tepid bath of shame, having not written *and* not rested and not gotten anything else done because I've been too busy piling on the negative self-talk.

A better scenario on a day like that would be, somewhere between coffee and eleven, I make a good-faith effort to try a few of my getting-unstuck tricks (such as the ones outlined earlier in this book), accept that writing is not going to happen today, and then do something *actually* restful, like reading a book, taking a nap, going for a walk, or sitting under a tree.

There are all kinds of theories about why it's so hard for us to really rest. There are neurological reasons (it's hard for our brains to transition from one state to another, from rest to work or from work to rest) and socioeconomic reasons (we may truly have very little time to rest because of having to work or take care of others). Some  reasons are based on ideas we get from our family and community and culture (we live in a culture in which measurable "productivity" is valued much more than rest). And technology has added another dimension to all of this (How do we turn ourselves "off" in an "always on" world?).

There aren't easy answers—not by a long shot. Some of the most revered thinkers of our day have tackled this question in books and articles and TED Talks for years and have still not come up with any great solution that works for everybody.

But in thinking about your own reality, are there ways to bring that hammock-reading-on-the-beach energy into *your* life when you need it?

For me, it starts with unplugging as much as possible. I turn my phone and every other connected device off, or put it in airplane mode, or set it to only let through the most important notifications. Sometimes I have to take drastic measures, like deleting social media apps or blocking myself from those sites.

That first step of unplugging, all by itself, starts to calm me. I breathe. I stretch. I think about what I really want to do with the next half hour or hour or afternoon, depending on how much time I have.

It might be something simple like getting under a fluffy blanket and reading a book, with no interruptions. No checking social media, and no taking a picture of myself under a fluffy blanket reading a book and tagging it #unplugged.

Just me and the book and the words in the book and the feeling of being warm and cozy.

Or maybe I have a different kind of energy, and my rest wants to be more active. A walk, for example. That also starts with unplugging. No pictures of the flowers or dogs I see on my walk. At the most, I'll listen to music, because sometimes music helps me feel more present, but no podcasts or books. I don't want anyone else's ideas or opinions in my head.

You might live in a place where it's not safe or convenient to take a walk, but you're not in a reading mood. Try to get comfortable somewhere inside and listen to music, if you can. Even if all you have is five or ten minutes, being still with your eyes closed and your ears open to some of your favorite music can be incredibly restful.

Connecting with your childhood self can be surprisingly restful, as well as absorbing. Was there something you loved doing when you were a kid, but you stopped doing it? Maybe it was

LEGOs or finger paints, Play-Doh or paper dolls, action figures or puzzles. If you still have any of those things around, dig them out of the closet and play. Maybe you have a favorite book from childhood nearby. Some of my most restful moments have involved paging through the few picture books I managed to hang onto from my childhood.

Another great option is to do nothing.

Yes, nothing.

Does that sound kind of boring?

Good!

Research suggests that boredom is one of the best things for your creative thinking processes.[1] Boredom is when our minds are free to wander because they aren't focused on tasks or reactions or stress. Boredom is a break from the information overload of social media feeds, news, advertisements.

This is when your unconscious thoughts can float into your consciousness, and those just might include new ideas for stories or cool videos or art projects, or new ways of thinking about old ideas you might be stuck on.

Try building some blocks of real rest and legit boredom into your life, a little at a time, and see where they take you!

5  Elpidorou, Andreas, "The Bright Side of Boredom," Frontiers in Psychology. https://www.frontiersin.org/articles/10.3389/fpsyg.2014.01245/full.

# Field Trip!

**"GET OUTSIDE. GET OUT INTO THE WORLD, MAN! YOU WANNA READ POETRY, LOOK AT THE STARS. LIGHT A CANDLE AND WRITE UNDER THE NEW MOON. THAT'S WHEN THE OPERATOR COMES TO WHISPER THE SECRET WORDS TO YOU."**
**—BOB DYLAN**

Chilling out and letting yourself get good and bored and quiet is one way of filling up your creative tank, but there are more active ways too that energize creative thinking when you're in a slump or can light new sparks if you're searching for ideas about what to do next.

Julia Cameron, author of *The Artist's Way*, popularized the concept of the "Artist Date." She describes it as:

> *a once-weekly, festive, solo expedition to explore something that interests you. The Artist Date need not be overtly "artistic"—think mischief more than mastery. Artist Dates fire up the imagination. They spark whimsy. They encourage play.*[6]

I like to think of it even more loosely, because for me the word *festive* is a lot of pressure! It takes a *lot* for me to feel "festive" or to engage in "mischief," and I am even afraid of the commitment

6  *Julia Cameron,* The Artist's Way *(New York: TarcherPerigree, 2016), 18.*

of doing it once a week. That's just my personality. I'm not a "seize the day" kind of personality. I'm a bit more cautious.

Because an "Artist Date" has all those associated pressures for me, I like to think of it as going on a visit with the world, or on a field trip. In fact, an "Artist Date" is very much like a school field trip. It's something different from the normal schedule, something special.

It's super easy to get into a rut of moving your body from one building to another, with brief interruptions for sleep. School, home, sleep. School, home, sleep. Church, home, sleep. School, soccer field, home, sleep. School, work, gym, home, sleep.

Maybe you go to a few other places as part of your routine, but that's the thing—it's *routine*. Sometimes routines can be helpful, and sometimes they need disruption. When you walk by the same corner almost every day or drive on the same route or go to the same coffee shop, you can almost stop seeing those familiar things. And remember, seeing and noticing and *paying attention* are big parts of keeping the creative tank filled.

When was the last time you disrupted your routine?

Mixing it up can really get you thinking about new things, or about old things in new ways.

Whatever you call it—an Artist Date, a visit with the world, a field trip—or even if you don't give it a special name—it's about engaging your mind in ways it's not used to, engaging your body by moving it through new spaces, and keeping your curiosity awake.

So what does a personal field trip look like?

That all depends on what is accessible and affordable for you, and what's available in your reality. The only other limits are your imagination and willingness to try new things!

I'm a fan of doing things that are free or almost free, minus some bus fare or the price of a cup of coffee or tea. For example:

- I like going to a library I've never been to before, browsing the shelves (especially sections I don't normally visit), and pulling down anything that looks interesting until I've got a huge stack of books and magazines. Then I sit at a table or flop onto a couch and explore what's in that stack. I have no agenda or goal while I'm doing this other than to engage with something new and spend time in a new environment.

- I love animals, so going someplace where I can watch animals is always rewarding. This could be a nearby dog park, a cat café, an animal adoption agency where they let you play with the kittens, or even a park that attracts wild birds along with people walking their dogs. It rekindles my wonder of the natural world.

- Sometimes I try to think ahead and find out if there are any free or reduced-admission days at museums in my area. Many museums have one day a month or even one day a week with free or reduced-price admission. Try searching "free stuff to do near me," and see what you discover!

- Walking around any neighborhood I rarely go to is one of my favorite free things to do. I like looking at houses I've never seen, and discovering little stores and parks I didn't know existed. It feels like I'm traveling to a totally different city or state even though it may only be ten minutes from my house.

- Another idea is to check for local arts-and-crafts fairs or farmers markets and spend part of a day wandering through, looking at all the booths and the variety of things you might never be interested in owning or making but can imagine someone who would. These are great places to people-watch and practice your curiosity about those who are different from you. Pick someone out of the crowd, and try to imagine what their house looks like, what they eat for breakfast, what kind of job they have. Stretch out your imagination.

- Many cities and towns have at least a few historic sites— that is, buildings or parks or places where something historically significant happened: a battle, a declaration, a strike, an accident, a discovery. It's usually free to go to these sites, and you can look online before or after your visit to learn background information. If you also search "walking tour" for the site or area or neighborhood, you can often find a free map to help you get the most out of it.

- Go to an art gallery! Many towns have "gallery strolls" where, one night a month, all the art galleries stay open late and you can check them all out. These are free events, and you're not expected to buy anything. It's like going to a lot of little free museums.

- If you have a camera or a phone with a camera, go out on a photography field trip. Take a hundred photographs of things interesting to you. Or search for "photo scavenger hunt" and see how many things on the list you can get a picture of.

If you've got some money to spend, here are more options:

- Check out an aquarium, aviary, animal sanctuary, or zoo. If you're not that into animals, these are still great spots for watching people.

- Go to a play or concert. If you've never been to a stage play or a classical music concert, it's an experience worth having at least once. You might feel very bored and antsy. If that happens and you can't stand it, you can always leave at intermission. No one will come after you and say you have to sit there the whole time, like they might on a school field trip. This is a *you* field trip!

- Go to a museum. It might be a modern-art museum, a science museum, a history museum, or even some very specific museum near your town. Are you lucky enough to live near the UFO Museum, the Museum of Miniatures, or the Bigfoot Discovery Museum? I'm jealous.

- Take a one-night class or workshop. For example, there's a local grocery store chain near me that regularly puts on a cooking night where you learn to make a specific dish. Some pottery and painting studios also let you take part in events like this.

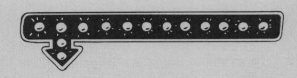

*BUDDY UP!*

*Julia Cameron, who coined the term "Artist Date," emphasizes that they are meant to be solo—a chance for you to connect with yourself, take your self out on a date. But depending on how old you are, how safe your town is, what your family rules are, and how confident you are about going out alone, it might be a good idea to go with a buddy.*

*What makes a good field trip buddy?*

*Someone who understands the point of it—to get out of your normal routine, engage with something new, and really pay attention to it. So, if you go to a new coffee shop with a friend, but you end up sitting there talking with each other about the same stuff you always talk about, or you get into looking at your phones, it's not really accomplishing the aspect of recharging yourself creatively.*

*Someone who is open to new things. We've all been in the situation of being out somewhere with a person who complains the whole time when things don't go according to plan or something makes them uncomfortable. That person would not be the perfect field trip buddy!*

*Someone who is also interested in creativity. Who better to be a creative field trip buddy than someone else who is also interested in writing, art, video, photography, or dance? You can support each other and take turns picking what to do on field trip days!*

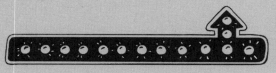

# Do Something You Are Very Bad At

You know what's fun? Doing stuff you're terrible at.

Just kidding! It's actually awful! But it can be good for your creative process.

I am very, *very* into being good at things. I don't enjoy doing things I'm bad at. One time, I took a neighborhood pottery class, thinking, *This will be a fun creative thing to do! There will be no pressure, just me and the clay*. But also what I thought was, *I'll probably be really good at this.*

I'd seen people make pottery on a pottery wheel, and when they were doing it, it looked super-duper easy and fun and cool. Throw some clay on there, spin the wheel, run your hands over the clay a few minutes and voilà, a vase! A bowl! A mug!

Well. What I discovered in the pottery class is that MAKING POTTERY IS EXTREMELY HARD FOR ME.

I couldn't center the clay on the pottery wheel. You're pressing a pedal with your foot to spin the wheel at the same time as you're trying to center the clay, which in itself is difficult. And the centrifugal force is working against you, and meanwhile as you wrestle with the clay, it dries out, and then it's like sandpaper is spinning in your bare hands at high speeds!

It would be nice to say that I was thinking, *Progress, not perfection. It's okay to be new at something*. It would be nice to say how I learned a valuable lesson about expectations and making peace with failure. It would be nice to say that this story had a heroic ending, with me tapping into the fun of learning something new and rejoicing in small steps.

Nope.

It ended with me saying a bunch of swears under my breath, walking out of the room in tears, and trying not to punch the wall.

But I went back the next week, and all the other weeks. I'd already paid for the whole class. Yet I refused to face my mortal enemy, the pottery wheel. The one thing I finished on the wheel that first night turned into a weird flat dish with a crooked, sharp point in the middle that I told everyone was for juicing lemons. I worked around the wheel and I learned other methods of making pottery that didn't involve using the wheel, and when the class was all over, I had several little pots with different colored glazes on them. They were . . . *not* good.

And then I never did pottery again, yay!

So, if it was so bad and I never did it again, why exactly am I recommending this?

"Getting out of your comfort zone" might be an overused phrase, but . . . sometimes you gotta get out of your comfort zone.

All of us are bad at something. Especially new things. And doing something you're not good at artistically is a way to practice imperfection and stretch yourself. For me it turned out that I didn't like pottery enough to keep doing it, but I had signed up because I thought I *might* really like it, and it was worth trying. Because another possible outcome was that I would enjoy it, get better, and learn something. You never know until you try. And trying is a great low-risk, low-stakes way to goof around creatively. You'll either come out with a new interest, or you'll hate the new thing and really appreciate the main thing that you love.

# Talking Back to the Voices in Your Head

**"REGARDLESS OF YOUR FIELD OF ARTISTIC ENDEAVOR, IT IS GOING TO COME DOWN TO CONFIDENCE (OR COURAGE, WHICH I USE INTERCHANGEABLY WITH CONFIDENCE). REMEMBER THAT YOU HAVE TAKEN YOURSELF OUT ONTO THIS LIMB BECAUSE YOU HAD SOMETHING TO SHOW THE WORLD. YOU HAVE A SINGULAR VISION, A SINGULAR SOUND, AND IT DESERVES TO BE HEARD. THERE WILL BE PLENTY OF VOICES (MOST PROMINENTLY, YOUR OWN) TRYING TO TELL YOU OTHERWISE. IT IS NOT RUDE FOR YOU TO TELL THE VOICES (YES, INCLUDING YOUR OWN) TO SHUT UP."**
*—CHRIS LYNCH, AUTHOR*

No matter how much creative practice you get, how self-aware you are, how many hours and years you accumulate of playing, making, and sharing, no matter how good you get at sorting the good advice from the bad . . . sometimes the negative chatter in your mind is still going to show up. I don't know why, but it's just how it is.

How much you listen to it and engage with it is up to you. Sometimes I ignore those voices, and sometimes I talk back. If there's chatter in your own mind trying to thwart you, it can be helpful (and even fun!) to write it out in dialog in your notebook or journal. This kind of self-talk can disempower the fears and remind you they're not in charge—you are. For example:

### *A CONVERSATION WITH FEAR*

> *YOU:*
> *Hey it's four p.m. Isn't this the time I said I was going to spend 25 minutes on my project?*
>
> *FEAR:*
> *(Cautiously) Yyyeahhh?*
>
> *YOU:*
> *So I want to work on it.*
>
> *FEAR:*
> *Um, I don't think that's a good idea right now.*
>
> *YOU:*
> *Why not?*
>
> *FEAR:*
> *Actually, it sounds pretty hard, is all.*
>
> *YOU:*
> *Yeah, it might be kind of hard.*
>
> *FEAR:*
> *Too hard.*
>
> *YOU:*
> *I mean, I don't think it'll be too hard.*
>
> *FEAR:*
> *It will. It will definitely be too hard. I hope you didn't tell anyone you were doing this.*
>
> *YOU:*
> *I told a couple of people . . .*
>
> *FEAR:*
> *OH NO, WHY, WHY WOULD YOU DO THAT???*
>
> *YOU:*
> *Actually, I thought—*

*FEAR:*
*This is so embarrassing. I'm getting a weird feeling in
my stomach just thinking about it.*

*YOU:*
*Calm down. It's fine.*

*FEAR:*
*I have to go lie down now. Where's my blankie?*

*YOU:*
*Okay, go ahead. I got stuff to do. See you after!*

## A CONVERSATION WITH SELF-DOUBT

*YOU:*
*Yay, time to work on my project!*

*SELF-DOUBT:*
*Oooh, your "project"? You're just so "artsy." Yeah, go work on
your "project!"*

*YOU:*
*Are you . . . dunking on me right now?*

*SELF-DOUBT:*
*I'm just saying you sound kind of stuck up.*

*YOU:*
*Because I want to do something creative?*

*SELF-DOUBT:*
*You think you're too good to just sit and watch TV?*

*YOU:*
*I . . .*

*SELF-DOUBT:*
*I mean, who told you that you have any talent? It's kind of a
joke.*

*YOU:*
*No, it's—*

*SELF-DOUBT:*
*"Look at me, I'm Sara and I'm 'working on my project'!"*
*Little Miss Artist, oh brother. You think you're better than*
*everyone. You think you're soooo special.*

*YOU:*
*Well, I'm a little special. Also, I never—*

*SELF-DOUBT:*
*Look, you don't know what you're doing, and no one cares if*
*you do it or not.*

*YOU:*
*I care!*

*SELF-DOUBT:*
*Oh, you care. Fine, if you want to waste your time, go ahead.*

*YOU:*
*Okay, I will! Also: shut up and leave me alone.*

### A CONVERSATION WITH DISTRACTION

*YOU:*
*Giddyup, it's time to CREATE!*

*DISTRACTION:*
*Yay! Oh, but first, did you see this video of the cat that*
*plays piano?*

*YOU:*
*I've seen it.*

*DISTRACTION:*
*No, it's a new one!*

*YOU:*
*I'll look later.*

*DISTRACTION:*
*Fine, but you should probably check the news before you start.*

*YOU:*
*Why?*

*DISTRACTION:*
*In case something bad happened! Or something interesting!*

*YOU:*
*What if it did? It will still be there in half an hour when I'm done.*

*DISTRACTION:*
*Let's get a snack real quick. It will help your concentration.*

*YOU:*
*Not really!*

*DISTRACTION:*
*I bet a lot of people liked your last tweet.*

*YOU:*
*Maybe.*

*DISTRACTION:*
*But if you look now, you'll know. Then you can forget about it!*

*YOU:*
*It . . . doesn't work that way.*

*DISTRACTION:*
*Have you ever thought about being a professional snowboarder?*

*YOU:*
*Go to your room.*

**"EVERY TIME YOU SIT UP STRAIGHT, CLOSE YOUR EYES, AND SPEND TEN MINUTES CLEARING YOUR MIND OF THOUGHT, YOUR NERVOUS SYSTEM CALMS DOWN JUST THE TINIEST BIT. LIKE DOING REPS OF PUSHUPS, YOU'LL BE BAD AT FIRST, BUT THESE BITS WILL ACCUMULATE OVER TIME UNTIL YOU'RE ABLE TO SIT DOWN WITHOUT YOUR HEAD BUZZING LIKE A CHAINSAW AND SEE YOUR WRITING AND A WAY THROUGH ALL OF ITS TANGLES AND KNOTS WITH A LOT MORE CLARITY."**

**–CHRISTIAN MCKAY HEIDICKER, WRITER**

# In Conclusion . . . For Now

**An excerpt from my journal, sometime in 2019:**

*As I write this, I am sitting in the living room of a vacation rental I can't really afford. It's a drizzly morning but I have the patio door open and I can hear the ocean—nature's white-noise machine—in the background. When I look out the window, I see a slate footpath, cypress trees, and, beyond those, the gray-green waves.*

*Renting this place for a few days was meant to trick me into working on what is supposed to be the final draft of a novel I have under contract. It's the fourth draft of what's been a years-long project, and though I've gone through this six times before and always come out at the end with a finished book, I'm terrified.*

*This time, I'm sure I won't be able to do it.*

*This time, I will be caught and everyone will know I'm a fraud.*

*This time will be the final nail in the coffin of my career, which was fake news all along.*

When people ask me what I do for a living and I tell them I write novels, the response is often something like "How fun!"

*Mmm,* I nod. *Fun.*

"I'm lucky," I say. That part is true. I am *very*, very lucky that I have gotten to do this as more or less my living for the last dozen or so years. But *fun* is not the word I would necessarily use, any more than I would use that word about life in general. Sometimes writing, like life, is fun. And sometimes writing, like life, is challenging in all sorts of ways.

For example, throughout the process of making this book, I've experienced the irony of being insecure and afraid as I write about creating courageously. Anytime I put myself forward as an expert, the resistance, the procrastination, the fear of failure, and the self-doubt all show up for the party.

I've been at this long enough to know that my own creative practice is probably always going to be like that for me: a mix of fun, fear, and hard work.

If it's not "fun" most of the time, if it stirs up my insecurity, if it leaves me fearful and exposed—sometimes to the point of tears— why do I do it?

Because I have always wanted to. Because the human brain is a storymaker. Because I understand myself and the world by making stuff up. Because when I don't do it, I don't feel like myself. Because enjoying or being touched by a work of art or creation makes me want to respond with another work of creation.

Because life can't be *all* making money, paying bills, social media, politics, homework, doing dishes, and worry.

There's something *more* here. Something alive and big and wild as the ocean outside my door when I wrote that journal entry, that I want to be a part of somehow. And being a part of it means answering it with my *yes* or my *no*, or with my *Here is how I see things,* with my *I'm here too.*

There's something in me always longing, always reaching out, and it isn't satisfied by just being part of the capitalism machine or the daily to-do lists of survival.

If you're reading this book, I bet you feel it too.

Yet no matter how powerful that longing is for us, that drive to speak out, to answer art with art, longing with longing, creation with creation—when the moment comes to *do* it, when *now* is *here*, there always seems to be a force waiting in the wings that says:

*Later. Don't. Can't.*

*What do you know?*

*No one cares; don't bother.*

*You're no good; your ideas are dumb; the work is pointless.*

*You're not talented enough, not smart enough. At least not as good or smart as* _____ [that person you want to be like].

*It's too hard.*

*You don't have what it takes; you're too lazy; you're too scared.*

*You are a coward.*

I know I have to meet that force with my courage, for all the reasons stated above and throughout this book, and most of all because of my belief that the very act of being alive is a continual act of creation.

No one has lived our lives before, and no one will again. That is a wondrous and often daunting challenge, and we reach for our courage not only in the moments of doing art or writing stories or singing our songs, but in so many other moments too. In this moment, and the next and the next and the next and the next and the next, when we are the ones to answer each question and accusation of that negative force:

Now. Will. Can.

I know what I know, and I know I keep learning.

*I care.*

I'm good enough because I *am.* My work and life have meaning, whatever I'm doing. I might be scared, and I might even be a coward sometimes when it comes to facing this act of creation that is life, and all the small acts of creation that happen within it. I can make the choice to curl up and hide sometimes, but that doesn't satisfy me for long. The fear and the discomfort are part of what it means to be alive. So is fun; so is joy. It all seems to come tied together, in the creative process and in life.

That longing to reach out and give our *yes* and *no* and *Here is how I see things* to life is embodied in the act of creation. We're in an ongoing call-and-response with life, whether we're making a poem, making a painting, making a song, making a book, making a movie, or simply waking up in the morning to start a new day in which we say:

*I'm here too.*

# For Further Reading

**Books:**

*The Artist's Way* – Julia Cameron

*The Creative Habit: Learn It and Use It for Life* – Twyla Tharpe

*Naming the World: And Other Exercises for the Creative Writer* – edited by Bret Anthony Johnston

*Becoming a Writer* – Dorothea Brande

*Bird by Bird: Some Instructions on Writing and Life* – Anne Lamott

*642 Things to Draw: Inspirational Sketchbook to Entertain and Provoke the Imagination*

*642 Things to Write About* – from the San Francisco Writers Grotto

**Websites:**

Screenwriting.io: answering basic questions about screenwriting https://screenwriting.io

Brain Pickings: brainpickings.org

Story a Day writing prompts: storyaday.org

Poets & Writers prompts: https://www.pw.org/writing-prompts-exercises

ArtPrompts prompt generator: artprompts.org